AUTOMOBILES
OF THE
'50s

Publications International, Ltd.

CONTENTS

Louis Weber, C.E.O.
Publications International, Ltd.
7373 North Cicero Avenue
Lincolnwood, Illinois 60646

Permission is never granted for commercial purposes.

Manufactured in U.S.A.

8 7 6 5 4 3 2

ISBN: 0-7853-2008-3

INTRODUCTION

Most of us tend to look back fondly on our youth. We're only young once, after all, and over time we tend to remember the good and forget the bad. Those are the main reasons why American automobiles of the Fifties still command such high interest among the millions of forty- and fiftysomethings who grew up with them.

But how to explain the equally strong fascination post-Kennedy generations have for these cars? The answer, quite simply, is that for those people, as well as for many of today's aging baby boomers, the cars of Fifties Detroit evoke the period as vividly as hula hoops, Elvis, and *Leave It to Beaver*.

The Fifties were not the best of times for America, but they were hardly the worst. Yes, the Soviet Union *did* seem an "evil empire" then, and we rushed to build backyard fallout shelters to defend against atomic attack. We worried, too, about losing a "space race" once Russia launched its *Sputnik* as the first artificial Earth satellite in 1957. In 1950-53 we fought North Korea and Red China to a draw on the Korean peninsula, following President Truman's policy to contain Communism anywhere in the world. Meantime, the demagogic senator Joe McCarthy and others here at home began ferreting out a "Red menace" they mainly imagined. Down South, cries for overdue racial equality began rising in marches, sit-ins, and "freedom rides."

But for most Americans the Fifties brought a sense of security and unprecedented prosperity. Having won World War II, we comforted ourselves by electing one of its greatest heroes, Dwight D. Eisenhower, our president in 1952. Science was delivering one breathtaking new wonder after another: the Salk polio vaccine, jet air travel, "hi-fi," and, of course, television. The boom in consumerism and industrial production was matched by a soaring postwar birth rate. American families indulged their taste for "the good life" with a cornucopia of colorful new gadgets—many of them fingertip-automatic, of course. The American Dream was a spiffy new split-level home in the suburbs with a shiny new car in the garage—maybe two. And for the first time in a generation, the dream was achievable by most everyone. Who could ask for anything more?

Certainly not Detroit. In the Fifties, America was absolute king of the automotive world; "import car" was as foreign a term as *Volkswagen*, and "Made in Japan" meant laughably cheap and shoddy. American cars reflected the unbridled national optimism of the day: longer-lower-wider each year, and usually heavier, shinier, and faster. But why not? Gas was only two bits a gallon, so buyers could afford performance. Detroit happily obliged them by running a "horsepower race" (trumpeted with optimistic SAE gross horsepower figures, cited throughout this book). By mid-decade, the compact high-compression V-8 was the public's engine of choice, and woe be to those companies who didn't offer one.

The era brought other significant market trends. The pillarless coupe or "hardtop convertible," a late-Forties innovation, won universal acceptance in the Fifties. So, too, did the all-steel station wagon, which by late decade had cross-pollinated with the pillarless coupe in a spate of hardtop wagons. Fully automatic transmission became another hugely popular essential; if it worked by pushbuttons, all the better.

Other new automotive ideas were just dead ends. Air suspension was briefly tried, but proved unreliable in those pre-electronic years, and far too costly to find much favor. Ditto fuel injection, though it, too, would return some three decades later. A few automakers tried selling compact cars, but only Rambler (and some tiny imports in recessionary 1958) did good business in the "bigger is better" tenor of the times. Attempts at European-type sports cars fared no better; the now-legendary Corvette was born in the Fifties, but almost didn't survive them. Tailfin styling, tri-tone paint jobs, and swivel seats pandered to a public fondness for gadgets that evaporated almost with the decade itself. Catering to no one were soggy handling, dodgy brakes, and workmanship that ranged from suspect to awful (more typically the latter after about 1956).

Yet not all Fifties Detroiters were (as one observer termed them) "insolent chariots" thrown together with planned obsolescence in mind. Indeed, triumphs like the Continental Mark II and Chrysler 300 have long since become coveted collectibles. Other cars, like the heroically finned 1959 Cadillac, have come to symbolize an era that's unique in American history.

Whether your preferred Fifties car sums up wretched excess or is a timeless classic, you'll find it in *Automobiles of the '50s*, an authoritative year-by-year review of all major U.S. makes, including those that, regrettably, departed during the decade.

So whether you grew up with these cars or are just discovering them now, we hope you enjoy this historic ride down Memory Lane. As the beatniks, those hippies of the Fifties, would say, "It's a gas!"

1959 Edsel Corsair convertible coupe

Imagine Chrysler selling shirts, Ford merchandising mattresses, or GM hawking power tools. That may sound strange, but no more so than retailing giant Sears getting into the car business, which it did for a brief time in the Fifties.

The story begins in the late Forties with Theodore V. Houser, then vice-president of merchandising for Sears, Roebuck and also on the board of Kaiser-Frazer, the upstart postwar automaker. In 1949, Houser broached the idea of marketing a K-F product under Sears' familiar Allstate name—a complete car to be sold along with parts and accessories for it at the new auto shops then opening up adjacent to Sears' retail stores. A hookup with Kaiser-Frazer was a natural. At the time, Houser was buying Homart enamelware from Kaiser Metals Company, in which Sears held a 45-percent interest.

The first thought was simply to put Allstate logos on K-F's large 1949 models, but Sears was dubious. Then the compact Henry J came along in 1951 (see "Kaiser"), exactly the car Houser had been looking for: simple, inexpensive, and easy to service.

Somehow, K-F president Edgar F. Kaiser managed to convince his dealers to accept a chain department store as a competitor, and the Allstate was announced that November. It was the only new American make for 1952, and the first car Sears had offered since a high-wheeler 40 years before. In an apparent attempt to feel out the market, Sears initially concentrated promotion in the Southeast, though the Allstate was ostensibly available nationwide through the 1952 Sears catalog.

It was obviously a Henry J, but sported a distinctive front end designed by Alex Tremulis (recently associated with the Tucker fiasco), plus a major interior upgrade in line with Sears' policy of improving on proprietary products. K-F interior specialist Carleton Spencer used quilted saran plastic combined with a coated paper fiber encapsulated in vinyl, a material he'd discovered in use on the transatlantic telegraph cable. Seemingly impervious to normal wear, it was superior to the upholstery of most Henry Js.

Not surprisingly, Sears specified its own Allstate batteries, sparkplugs, and tube tires, each with the appropriate guarantee: 18 months for tires, 24 months on the battery, and 90 days/4000 miles for the vehicle itself (K-F's standard warranty). Allstates usually had trunklids and dashboard gloveboxes, items found less often on Henry Js, though the basic and standard-trim versions lacked the opening trunk. The costlier Deluxe Six had armrests and a horn ring, which weren't available on lesser versions even at extra cost.

Otherwise, everything else was the same. This meant KF's pudgy little two-door sedan with fastback styling, 100-inch wheelbase, and choice of two L-head Willys engines: a 134-cubic-inch four-cylinder with 68 horsepower or a 161-cid 80-bhp six. Sears' marketing was more aggressive, though, with five Allstate models to Henry J's four. The cheapest '52 Allstate, the basic Four, was priced at $1395, just below the standard Henry J.

There was little change for '53. A full-width rubber-

1952 Allstate Four two-door sedan

1952 Allstate Four two-door sedan

covered pad was added to the instrument panel, taillights were relocated to the rear fenders, and models reduced to two Fours and the Six.

But by then, it was clear that the idea had failed. Whether it was because people didn't take to buying cars in department stores or because of the narrow marketing approach is difficult to determine. Both factors probably contributed. Only 1566 Allstates were built for 1952. The count was 797 when Sears canceled the project in early '53, leaving plans for future models stillborn. Among these was a pair of proposals for a two-door station wagon, one by industrial designer Brooks Stevens, the other by Gordon Tercey of K-F Styling.

Allstates are extremely rare today, and thus more desired than comparable Henry Js by collectors. In 1971, Allstate Insurance purchased an Allstate car for historical purposes. In the Sixties it would have been hard to convince the folks behind Sears parts counters that the car had ever existed.

ALLSTATE AT A GLANCE				
Model Year	1950	1951	1952	1953
Price Range, $			1395-1693	1528-1785
Weight Range, Lbs.			2300-2355	2405-2455
Wheelbases, Ins.			100	100
4 Cyl. Engines, BHP			68	68
6 Cyl. Engines, BHP			80	80

Buicks of the Fifties were a lot like their owners: successful upper-middle-class types with a bit too much girth and, at times, way too much flash, but always substantial and mostly predictable. This was a successful era for General Motors' Flint division, highlighted by record sales through mid-decade and, for 1953, a 50th anniversary celebrated with the make's first ever V-8. Yet the traditional foundations of Buick success remained unaltered: quality, high performance for the price, and products carefully orchestrated to fit the times and market.

Depending on your point of view, Buick's Fifties styling reflected either the best contemporary thinking or the worst depravity of those glittery years before compacts, emission controls, and safety regulations. But one thing was undeniable: The massive postwar restyling that affected all GM makes for 1948-49 had produced the lowest, sleekest Buicks in history. And, of course, there was more to come. If '49 had been the "Year of the Porthole," 1950 was the "Year of the Sweepspear." Both would remain Buick hallmarks through the Fifties and beyond.

Buick entered the decade with its well-established lineup of Specials, Supers, and Roadmasters, which would persist through 1953. All wore a new look for 1950, dominated by big, toothy vertical-bar grilles and fuller body contours, styling that would also persist through 1953.

Specials of this period strode a half-inch longer, 121.5-inch wheelbase, but remained competitively priced cars designed to catch third-place Plymouth in the sales race. The 1950 series comprised standard and Deluxe trim spread among fastback and "Touring" notchback 4-doors, fastback "sedanet" coupe, and a revived business coupe, all a bit utilitarian. Later, the sedanet was the only "jetback" model for '51, when the Special received its own version of Buick's pioneering 1949 Riviera hardtop coupe, which had spread to the Super series for 1950.

The Riviera name also graced a well-proportioned four-door sedan offered for 1950-51 in Roadmaster and Super guise, with special extended wheelbases (130.3 and 125.5 respectively). Both lines also included woody Estate Wagons through '53, with structural body parts of mahogany and white ash. They were big, expensive haulers: The '53 Roadmaster Estate cost a hefty $4031 and weighed 4315 pounds.

Super remained Buick's volume seller in these years despite few offerings: just standard and Riviera sedans, convertible, Riviera hardtop, and Estate, plus a 1950 sedanet and a handful of notchback 1952 two-door sedans. Roadmaster body styles essentially duplicated Super's.

Buick continued to rely on an aging but proven valve-in-head straight eight for all its 1950-52 models and the '53 Special. Displacement, compression, and horsepower varied. The 1950 Special engine was a 248 cubic-incher producing 115 standard horsepower or 120 with Dynaflow Drive, a Special option through the end of the series in 1958. Supers and 1951-53 Specials used a 263-cid version with horsepower as high as 128. Roadmasters used a hefty 320 that by 1952 was developing 170 bhp at 3800 rpm.

Dynaflow—some called it "Dynaslush"—was Buick's pioneering torque-converter automatic transmission first offered as a Roadmaster option for 1948. It then became standard there, and an increasingly popular extra for other models at around $200. It multiplied torque via a drive turbine induced to rotate through an oil bath by a facing crankshaft-driven turbine. Dynaflow was smooth, but none too exciting for performance. The Twin-Turbine Dynaflow of 1953 was more positive in operation. By decade's end, an even better Triple-Turbine unit was offered across the board as a $296 option. But Dynaflow in any form couldn't deliver acceleration like Hydra-Matic, and was therefore handicapped in an age of horsepower and hot rods.

Golden Anniversary 1953 brought first-time availability of power steering, a 12-volt electrical system, and a fine new overhead-valve V-8 for Super and Roadmaster. An oversquare design of 322 cid (bore and stroke: 4.00 × 3.25 inches), this new "Fireball" engine offered up to 188 bhp on an industry-topping 8.5:1 compression ratio. Roadmasters were demoted to the 121.5-inch wheelbase save the Riviera sedan, which now shared the 125.5-inch chassis of the counterpart Super.

Buick's 50th year also brought a flashy new limited-

1950 Buick Super convertible

1950 Buick Roadmaster Riviera four-door sedan

edition sports convertible. Called Skylark, it was perfect for Hollywood types and Texas oil barons. But that wasn't why only 1690 were built. The reason was price: an extraordinary $5000.

Skylark was one of those special projects for which GM design chief Harley Earl had long been famous. Carefully concocted for the broadest possible appeal, it was not a two-seat sports car—which then accounted for only 0.27 percent of the market—but a luxurious, sporty "personal" four-seater like Ford's post-1957 Thunderbirds. Like 1953's similar Oldsmobile Fiesta and Cadillac Eldorado, the debut Skylark was basically a chopped-and-sectioned version of Buick's regular ragtop. But though trimmed

like a Roadmaster, it looked much cleaner and more rakish, with a four-inch lower windshield, no portholes, fully radiused rear-wheel openings, and standard Kelsey-Hayes chrome wire wheels, then becoming fashionable throughout the industry.

Like Olds and Cadillac, Buick adopted longer and more massively square bodies for 1954, but also revived its prewar "factory hot rod" with a new Century series offering the bigger Buick engine in the smaller Buick body. All models wore inverted-U grilles with fine vertical bars set under oval nacelles cradling headlamps and parking lamps. Windshields were newly wrapped in the manner of recent GM showmobiles, and rear fenders

1951 Buick Roadmaster Estate station wagon

1951 Buick Roadmaster Riviera four-door sedan

1952 Buick Roadmaster Riviera hardtop coupe

1952 Buick Special two-door sedan

1953 Buick Roadmaster Estate station wagon

1953 Buick Skylark convertible

kicked up to mount vertical pairs of bullet taillamps high in their trailing edges. Offerings were regrouped to include a convertible, Riviera hardtop coupe, and 4-door sedan in all four series. Century and Special also offered new all-metal 4-door Estate Wagons (remarkably with no ersatz wood trim). A 2-door Sedan was exclusive to Special, and the price-leader of the line at $2207.

Special belatedly received its own Fireball V-8 for '54, a 264-cid unit with 143/150 bhp. Other models carried the 322 with power ratings of 177 (manual-shift Century) to 200 (Roadmaster and Skylark). Wheelbases were again realigned: 122 inches for Special/Century, 127 for Super/Roadmaster.

The Skylark was back for '54, but much less a "custom" than the '53, though that enabled Buick to cut its price to $4483. Now more Century than Roadmaster, it stood apart with tack-on tailfins and huge chrome-plated die-cast taillight housings, plus the circular rear-wheel openings. Overall, it somewhat resembled Buick's '54 Wildcat II show car, but was evidently less impressive than the '53 Skylark, for only 836 were sold before the model was dropped (in favor of the Century wagon).

Much of Buick's '54 styling had already been previewed by the XP-300 and 1951 LeSabre show cars, rolling testbeds for a number of new ideas. Both used an experimental 215-cid aluminum V-8, which wasn't a forerunner of Buick's identically sized early-Sixties engine but was quite special all the same. With exactly square dimensions (3.25-inch bore and stroke), 10:1 compression and Roots-type supercharger, it produced over 300 bhp—phenomenal for the day. Only trouble was, it had to run on a combination of methanol and gasoline, not exactly common at local filling stations.

Both these showpieces were futuristic. The 116-inch-wheelbase LeSabre sported a wrapped windshield and "Dagmar" bumpers. The XP-300, measuring an inch less between wheel centers, had the mesh-backed headlamp nacelles that would appear on production '54s.

Speaking of which, Buick had been pushing relentlessly toward the industry's number-three spot. It broke an all-time record in calendar 1950 with more than 550,000 cars. The '54 tally of 531,000 left Buick trailing only Chevrolet and Ford, a position it hadn't held since 1930. Buick set another calendar-year record for 1955 at 781,000, nearly 50 percent higher than its previous best.

This success was largely due to the Special, which supplanted Super as the most popular Buick after 1953. It was also one of the most popular cars in all Detroit. Over 380,000 were built for 1955, the industry's banner year of the decade, including 155,000 Riviera two-door hardtops, that season's single most popular Buick. A deft restyle for '55 only kept division sales booming, aided by even more potent Fireball V-8s delivering 188 bhp on Specials, 236 bhp elsewhere.

Mid-model year '55 brought four-door Riviera hardtop sedans to the Special and Century series; Super and Roadmaster versions followed for '56. Once more, the rest of the industry had to play catch-up with a GM innovation (this one initially shared with Oldsmobile).

1954 Buick Century Estate station wagon

1954 Buick Roadmaster convertible

1955 Buick Special four-door sedan

1955 Buick Roadmaster Riviera hardtop coupe

The '56 Buicks didn't sell as well as the '55s, but then '56 was a "breather" for most of the industry. Another facelift brought model-year designation to exterior nameplates, a practice Buick would abandon after 1957 amid customer complaints that it made their cars obsolete that much sooner.

Meantime, a "horsepower race" was on all over Detroit, so the '56s were the most powerful Buicks yet. The Special's 264 V-8 was up to 220 bhp; the rest of the line boasted 322s with 255 bhp. A Century could now leap from 0-60 mph in 10.5 seconds and top 110.

Longer and lower new bodies arrived for '57, along with a slightly more exaggerated version of '56 styling. Though division general manager Ed Ragsdale never said how much this makeover cost, it must have run several hundred million. Yet despite the most sweeping alterations since 1949, the '57s didn't sell particularly well, mainly because rivals were pressing GM hard for industry design leadership. Chrysler, in fact, took over for '57 with its all-new line of longer, much lower, glassier, and dramatically more tailfinned cars created under Virgil Exner.

1956 Buick Century convertible

1957 Buick Roadmaster 75 Riviera hardtop sedan

1957 Buick Century Riviera hardtop coupe

1958 Buick Limited convertible coupe

1958 Buick Special four-door sedan

1959 Buick LeSabre four-door sedan

Still, Flint's '57s were dashing and fairly clean for the period. And horsepower was the highest yet: 250 for Special, an even 300 elsewhere, thanks to a bore/stroke job (from 4.00 × 3.20 to 4.13 × 3.40 inches) taking displace-ment out to 364 cubes.

Model changes for '57 were few but interesting: pillarless Caballero four-door wagons for Century and Special, and a new Series 75 Roadmaster offering Riviera hardtop coupe and sedan. The latter, essentially an upmarket version of the regular Series 70, had every possible standard luxury save air conditioning: Dynaflow, power steering and brakes, dual exhausts, automatic windshield washers, backup lights, clock, special interior with deep-pile carpeting, and a host of others. But though 1957 was a good year for Buick, it was even better for Plymouth, which pushed Flint from third back to fourth place in sales.

Things were even worse for 1958, notable for the ugliest Buicks in history. From contrived chrome-draped fins to a monstrous grille holding 160 shiny little squares, the "B-58" Buicks were awful—especially the heroically overdecorated Limited, a name revived from prewar times for a new series above Roadmaster. These were also the fattest Buick since the war—some 400 pounds heavier than the 1950 models and three-four inches longer than the '57s—yet performance suffered as horsepower was unchanged.

No '58 Buick sold well, though the year's "flash" recession was probably more to blame than the ghastly styling. Model-year production stopped at some 240,000 units, and Flint fell behind Oldsmobile to fifth in sales. Air suspension was offered, but seldom ordered. In all, '58 was a very bad year for Buick.

So was 1959. But if the '58s were tasteless, the '59s were just the opposite. Though dominated by the omnipresent tailfin—now bigger than ever and newly canted—the '59s were at least smooth, clean, and fairly dignified, with huge windshields and fewer chrome grille squares. Buick now shared the corporate A-body with other GM lines, but it wasn't obvious. Nor was the fact that '59 styling was a hurry-up reply to Chrysler's hugely successful '57s. But thank goodness for it; originally, the '59s were to have been facelifted '58s.

For the first time in two decades, Buick retitled its series. Special became LeSabre, Century was renamed Invicta, and Super and Roadmaster were dubbed Electra

1959 Buick Electra 225 convertible

and Electra 225. The last two rode a 126.3-inch wheelbase, trimmed 1.2 inches from 1957-58. LeSabre and Invicta shared a 123-inch chassis and the previous Special/Century body styles, though hardtop wagons were dropped due to low sales. Electras were downpriced quite a bit from their '58 counterparts, spanning a $3800-$4300 range. Buick was called 1959's most changed car. The design changes were definitely for the better.

On the mechanical side, 1959 brought a new 401-cid V-8 with 325 bhp for the upper three series; LeSabre stayed with the last Special's 364, still at 250 bhp. Power brakes and steering were standard on Electras, a $150 option elsewhere. Air conditioning was $430 across the board. Air suspension (for the rear only) was still nominally available—and almost never ordered.

Significantly, Buick dealers sold more Opels than ever in 1959. The "captive import" from GM's German subsidiary had been assigned to Buick the previous year, and promptly grabbed an increasing number of customers growing weary of oversize, overweight automobiles. But Buick was already planning its own compact, and its star would rise again.

BUICK AT A GLANCE										
Model Year	**1950**	**1951**	**1952**	**1953**	**1954**	**1955**	**1956**	**1957**	**1958**	**1959**
Price Range, $	1803-3433	2046-3780	2115-3977	2197-5000	2207-4483	2233-3552	2357-3704	2596-4483	2636-5125	2740-4300
Weight Range, Lbs.	3615-4470	3600-4470	3620-4505	3675-4315	3690-4355	3715-4415	3750-4395	3955-4539	4058-4710	4159-4660
Wheelbases, Ins.	121.5-130.25	121.5-130.25	121.5-130.25	121.5-125.5	122-127	122-127	122-127	122-127.5	122-127.5	123-126.25
8 Cyl. Engines, BHP	115-152	120-152	120-170	125-188	143-200	188-236	220-255	250-300	250-300	250-325

Cadillac began reaching for U.S. luxury-car leadership in the Thirties, and clinched it for good in the Fifties. Symbolizing its achievement was the 1958 death of Packard, once America's premier prestige make, due to an over-long reliance on medium-price products and a crippling 1954 merger with troubled Studebaker. Lincoln would never threaten Cadillac's supremacy in the Fifties, owing to a more limited lineup. Nor would Chrysler, even after spinning off Imperial as a separate make after 1954.

Several developments in the Forties laid the foundation for Cadillac's high Fifties success. First, the division returned to prestige cars exclusively after 1940, abandoning its medium-price LaSalle once the luxury market recovered from its Depression-era doldrums. Then Cadillac landed a formidable one-two postwar punch: tailfin styling for '48, followed by a landmark new overhead-valve V-8 for 1949, when the division also pioneered (with Olds and Buick) the instantly popular new hardtop convertible body style. About all Cadillac needed in the Fifties were styling and features that pleased most buyers most of the time, which it delivered.

Initially sized at 331 cubic inches, the Cadillac V-8 was the product of 10 years research and experimentation. It was mainly engineered by Ed Cole, Jack Gordon, and Harry Barr, who aimed for less weight and higher compression (to take advantage of the higher-octane fuels promised after the war). This dictated the overhead valve arrangement, a stroke shorter than bore (3.63 inches, versus 3.81), compact wedge-shape combustion chambers, and "slipper" pistons. The last, developed by Byron Ellis, traveled low between the crankshaft counterweights, allowing for short connecting rods and low reciprocating mass.

With all this, the ohv arrived with 160 bhp, 10 more than Cadillac's last 346 L-head V-8—and from less displacement, testifying to its efficiency. The ohv had other advantages. Though built of cast iron, like the L-head, it weighed nearly 200 pounds less, yet would prove just as durable and reliable. Initial compression was only 7.5:1, yet could be pushed as high as 12:1; the L-head couldn't. The ohv also boasted more torque and 14-percent better fuel economy. Equally important, it had room enough to be greatly enlarged—as it soon was.

This superb engine combined with a surprisingly competent chassis to make early-Fifties Cadillacs some of the best road cars of that day. Chicago enthusiast Ed Gaylord, who backed the short-lived Gaylord car of mid-decade, owned a 1950 Series 61 with standard shift and 3.77 rear axle. He also had a new Jaguar XK-120 at the time. Gaylord later said that "the Cadillac was the faster car up to about 90 mph. [It also] set what was then a stock-car record at the original quarter-mile drag races in Santa Ana, California....The only competition I had in acceleration was from the small 135-horsepower Olds 88 coupe, but the Cadillac engine was substantially more efficient both in performance and economy." Indeed, such a car could clock 0-60 mph in around 13 seconds and easily top 100 mph.

1950 Cadillac Series Sixty-One Club Coupe

1952 Cadillac Series Sixty-Two Coupe de Ville hardtop

1953 Cadillac Series Sixty-Two Eldorado convertible coupe

1954 Cadillac Fleetwood Sixty Special four-door sedan

1955 Cadillac Series Sixty-Two convertible coupe

1956 Cadillac Series Sixty-Two Coupe de Ville hardtop

1957 Cadillac Eldorado Biarritz convertible coupe

1957 Cadillac Series Sixty-Two Sedan de Ville hardtop

Further proof of the V-8's prowess was provided by sportsman Briggs Cunningham, who entered a near-stock 1950 Cadillac in that year's 24 Hours of Le Mans in France. Driven by Sam and Miles Collier, it finished 10th overall—a performance unmatched by any other production luxury car—tearing down the Mulsanne Straight at around 120 mph and averaging 81.5 mph for the entire event. Cunningham himself drove a streamlined Cadillac-powered special that the French called Le Monstre. He went even faster than the Colliers, but lost top gear and finished right behind them. Perhaps most impressive, a British-built Allard J2, powered by the same Cadillac V-8, finished third.

Of course, such exploits mattered less in showrooms than the smooth, powerful V-8 itself. And Cadillac had another advantage going into the Fifties: GM's equally smooth and efficient self-shift Hydra-Matic Drive, by then standard on all models except the low-priced Series 61. Together with the V-8, it made for luxury-car performance demonstrably superior to that of rival heavyweights with less vigorous drivetrains. Though the V-8 would remain at 331 cid through 1955, it gained over 100 bhp in the interim, reaching 270 on that year's Eldorado.

Alas, Cadillac styling ultimately drifted to chrome-laden glitter, reaching a low point with the 1958-59 models. But the basic 1948 tailfinned design, inspired by wartime aircraft and originated by Franklin Q. Hershey under the watchful eye of GM design director Harley Earl, was good enough to remain largely intact through 1953. This was no real surprise. As Cadillac styling chief Bill Mitchell noted: "A traditional look is always preserved. If a grille is changed, the tail end is left alone; if a fin is changed, the grille is not monkeyed with."

And so it was: a new one-piece windshield, revamped grille, and a somewhat bulkier lower-body look for '50; small auxiliary grilles under the headlamps for '51; a winged badge in that spot for '52; one-piece rear windows and suggestive "Dagmar" bumper bullets for '53. A fairly important change is that, unlike sister GM divisions, Cadillac completely abandoned Forties-style fastbacks for 1950, switching pillared coupes to notchback profiles with hardtop-type rooflines inspired by the successful 1949 Coupe de Ville.

Otherwise, the Cadillac lineup didn't change much in this period. Still accounting for most sales, the Series 62 offered four-door sedan, pillared coupe, pillarless Coupe de Ville, and convertible, all on the usual 126-inch wheelbase. The familiar Sixty Special continued as a solitary super-luxury sedan on its own 130-inch platform (versus 133 inches in the Forties), while the Series 75 continued its traditional array of limousines and long owner-driver sedans on a 146.8-inch chassis. The Series 61, still the "entry-level" Caddy, was demoted to a 122-inch wheelbase (from 126), but again offered a sedan plus a newly styled deVille-inspired pillared coupe. Manual shift was standard on 61s, which were otherwise identical to 62s save chrome rocker moldings and slightly plainer interiors. Cadillac also continued supplying chassis for various coachbuilders, averaging about 2000 units per year through 1959.

Prices for the 1950 line started at $2761 for the Series 61 coupe (although few models went for under $3000) and reached up to about $5000 for a 75 sedan or limo. The 61s cost about $575 less than comparable 62s. But the division really didn't need a "price leader" anymore, so the 61s were dropped after 1951, never to return. Rival Packard, meantime, was still pushing cars priced up to $750 less than the Series 61s, a mistake that Packard didn't fully realize until too late.

Three GM divisions had 50th anniversaries in 1953, and celebrated by issuing expensive, flashy limited editions, all big convertibles with Motorama-inspired styling features. Buick offered the Skylark and Oldsmobile the 98 Fiesta. Cadillac's birthday model appeared in the Series 62 as the Eldorado. Only 532 were built that year, largely because of a towering $7750 price. Among its attractions: custom interior, special cut-down "Panoramic" wraparound windshield, sporty "notched" beltline, and a metal lid instead of a canvas boot to cover the lowered top. A striking piece, it was a preview of Cadillacs to come—and, of course, the start of a now long-famous line. Incidentally, some '53 Cadillacs were built with Buick Dynaflow after a fire in the Hydra-Matic plant at Willow Run reduced available transmission supplies, though this situation lasted only a few months.

Model year 1954 saw a major restyle and more power. A more squared-up look arrived on a longer, lower new GM C-body bearing the trendy wrapped windshield. Wheelbase lengthened to 129 inches on Series 62s, 133 on the Sixty Special, and 149.8 on 75s. V-8 power was booted to 230; power steering and windshield washers became standard. Four-way power seats were a new option.

Pillared coupes didn't return for '54, but Eldorado did. Though more like the standard Series 62 convertible, the '54 was far less expensive—$4738. Buyers responded, snapping up 2150. The figure improved to 3950 units for '55, then twice as many for '56, when Eldorados doubled to include a Seville hardtop coupe priced at the same $6556 as the retitled Biarritz convertible.

Eldorado was more distinctive again after '54, with sharply pointed "shark" fins above round taillights. Other models retained the small taillight-and-fin motif that had become a Cadillac hallmark. The division's basic '54 look persisted through effective, if evolutionary, facelifts for 1955 and '56. The latter year saw introduction of Cadillac's first four-door hardtop Sedan de Ville, which immediately scored almost as many sales as the Coupe de Ville and standard 62 hardtop combined.

Division sales, which had first topped 100,000 for 1950, continued upward, reaching 140,777 for '55. But even that was a temporary plateau. Despite an all-new '56 Lincoln and revitalized '57 Imperial, Cadillac remained America's luxury sales leader by far. Combined Lincoln/Imperial volume never exceeded 40,000 cars a year in this era; at Cadillac, that was good quarterly output.

Cadillac horsepower seemed to climb right along with sales. For 1955 it reached 250 standard via higher

1958 Cadillac Eldorado Brougham hardtop sedan

1958 Cadillac Series Sixty-Two Sedan de Ville hardtop

1959 Cadillac Sedan de Ville hardtop

1959 Cadillac Series Sixty-Two convertible coupe

compression (9.0:1) and improved manifolding; Eldorado now boasted 270 bhp courtesy of dual four-barrel carburetors, optional for other models. For 1956, the milestone V-8 was stroked to an even 4 inches to deliver 285 bhp standard and 305 for Eldorado.

The ratings were 300/325 for 1957, when compression went to 10:1 and the line was again rebodied, emerging with blockier but still evolutionary styling inspired by the Orleans, Eldorado Brougham, and Park Avenue show cars of 1954-55. Reaching into the luxury stratosphere, Cadillac unveiled a production Eldorado Brougham priced at a princely $13,074. Like its Motorama namesake, it was a surprisingly compact, low-slung pillarless sedan with a special 126-inch-wheelbase chassis, center-opening doors, and a brushed stainless-steel roof (one of Harley Earl's favorite touches). Standard quad headlights were an industry first shared that year with Lincoln, Nash, and some Chrysler Corporation cars.

The Brougham's most intriguing mechanical feature was its unique air suspension, the work of engineers Lester Milliken and Fred Cowin. Based on systems used for commercial vehicles since 1952, it employed an air "spring" at each wheel comprising a domed air chamber, rubber diaphragm, and pistons. Fed by a central air compressor, the domes were continually adjusted for load and road conditions via valves and solenoids for a smooth, level ride. Cadillac's system differed from "air ride" options at other GM divisions in being "open" (taking in air from outside) rather than "closed." Unhappily, cost and complexity were too high relative to benefits. The air domes leaked, and dealer replacements were frequent, leading many owners to junk the system in favor of conventional coil springs. Four years later, Cadillac and GM abandoned air suspension altogether.

After two years and 704 units, the Brougham was fully restyled and its final assembly farmed out to Pininfarina in Italy. Only 99 were built for '59, another 101 of the near-identical '60s. Though clean-looking (lines actually previewed Cadillac's 1961 styling), these were larger (130-inch wheelbase) and heavier cars that weren't put together very well (bodies contained lots of lead filler). They're collector's items now, but restoring one is a chore.

The volume Cadillacs were heavily facelifted for 1958 in a manner typical of GM that year. Perhaps the most garish Caddys yet, they were laden with chrome and far less stylish than previous postwar models. Sales were poor, though a nationwide recession was probably more to blame than the baroque styling, which was, after all, in vogue. At 121,778 units, model year production was lower than at any time since 1954. Symbolizing the fall in fortunes was a V-8 slightly detuned in a faint nod toward fuel economy, limited to a single 310-bhp version for all models.

Forecasting the future, DeVille became a 62 sub-series for '58, and pillared sedans were temporarily eliminated. The 62 line also gained a hardtop sedan with extended rear deck. All models were available with cruise control, high-pressure cooling system, two-speaker radio with automatic signal-seeking, and automatic parking brake release. A special show Eldorado introduced a "thinking" convertible top that raised itself and the side windows when a sensor detected raindrops, but this was another gimmick that came to nothing.

Another new C-body arrived for 1959, bringing far more curvaceous styling distinguished by huge windshields, thin-section rooflines, slim pillars—and soaring fins of ridiculous proportions, capped by bullet taillamps. But there were some worthy detail suspension changes and improved power steering, plus a V-8 stroked to 390 cid. Even better, the high-performance Eldorado engine was back, giving 345 bhp; other models were up to 325, which the Eldo had two years before.

DeVille now became a distinct series, offering hardtop sedans with flat-top four-window styling and a curvier six-window roofline, plus a hardtop coupe. The Series 62 duplicated these, and added a convertible. Still pillarless (as it had since been since '57), the lush Sixty Special now shared a new 130-inch wheelbase with all other standard models, including the line-topping Eldorado trio of Seville, Biarritz, and Brougham.

Prices were generally higher than before, with Series 62s at around $5000 and Eldos going for $7400 and up. Still, Cadillac built over 142,000 of its '59s, a fair gain on its 1958 showing. Though not appreciated then, these Caddys are now sought-after as the epitome of Fifties kitsch with their massive size, sparkling trim, and, especially, those overblown fins.

Despite a few lapses, the Fifties had been a great 10 years for Cadillac—the greatest ever in terms of expansion. A car for the very wealthy in 1950, Cadillac was solidly entrenched by decade's end among younger buyers on the way up.

CADILLAC AT A GLANCE										
Model Year	1950	1951	1952	1953	1954	1955	1956	1957	1958	1959
Price Range, $	2761-4959	2831-5405	3587-5643	3571-7750	3838-6090	3882-6402	4201-6828	4677-13,074	4784-13,074	4892-13,075
Weight Range, Lbs.	3822-4586	3807-4652	4140-4733	4225-4850	4365-4815	4358-5113	4420-5130	4565-5390	4630-5425	4690-5490
Wheelbases, Ins.	122-149.75	122-149.75	126-146.75	126-147	129-149.75	129-149.75	129-149.75	129-149.75	129.5-149.75	130-149.75
8 Cyl. Engines, BHP	160	160	190	210	230	250-270	285-305	300-325	310-325	325-345

CHECKER

Founded in 1922, Checker won fame for specially designed taxicabs and airport limousines, then began selling "civilian" models in 1959. Actually, some sources say the Checker catalog mentioned "pleasure car" versions as early as 1948, but the Kalamazoo factory always said 1959 was the first year for private (non-fleet) sales.

Assuming you could find a Checker dealer (they were never very numerous), you could buy what was initially called a Superba, offered as a four-door sedan and wagon in standard and Special trim. Specials were more deluxe inside, but not much. All were the same tank-like affairs familiar to anyone who ever hailed a Checker cab since the A8 model hit the streets in 1956. Wheelbase remained at 120 inches, fairly compact for the time. Curb weights ranged around 3400 pounds for sedans to nearly 3800 for wagons.

Morris Markin, Checker's founder and president, was steadfast: There'd be no change to this dumpy but practical design so long as there were buyers for reliable, durable "taxi-tough" cars. Not that there'd been many changes before. Aside from non-commercial paint jobs and leaving off the "hire light," the Superba differed from the A8 only in a front-end facelift with trendy quad headlamps and a checked (what else?) grille, though the taxis also had this from 1959.

Superba power came from Continental Motor Company, basically the same 226-cubic-inch L-head six that Kaiser had used. Here, though, it was available in side-valve and overhead-valve versions at no difference in price. The former had 7.3:1 compression and produced a mere 80 horsepower, so it must have been meant for areas where gas was of really poor quality. The ohv unit had more modern 8.0:1 compression and a more respectable 122 bhp. Transmissions were the expected three-speed column shift manual and bought-in Borg-Warner automatic.

True to its taxi traditions, the Superba sedan could be equipped with a pair of rear jump seats for carrying up to eight. The wagon had the same roomy back seat, plus roll-down tailgate window and a voluminous cargo deck. Dashboards were flat-faced and straightforward, with plain round gauges and plain-Jane looks right out of a '51 Plymouth.

But at a time when mainstream Detroiters rolled on 14-inch wheels, Checker stuck with 15s, which made for smoother taxi rides over the increasingly cratered streets of urban America. Also reflecting its taxi origins, the Superba featured tall doors and ruler-flat floors for easy entry/exit and plenty of foot space. It did not, however, feature much in the way of luxury: rubber mats where carpeting might have been, pedestrian hardboard headliner, and a conspicuous absence of late-Fifties safety features like padded dash and sunvisors, dished steering wheel, and seatbelts.

But civilian Checkers would be better equipped in later years, starting when the awkwardly named Superba became a Marathon in 1961. Yet despite that, and availability of lively Chevy V-8 power after 1964, Checker

Early '50s Checker taxicab four-door sedan

1953 Checker taxicab four-door sedan

1956-58 Checker A8 four-door sedan

sales would always be modest at most through 1970. Then began a slow, steady decline that proved irreversible. Checker finally ceased production in mid-1982, a victim of drastically changed world economics, high overhead, and stronger Big Three competition.

CHECKER AT A GLANCE	
Model Year	**1959**
Price Range, $	2540-3005
Weight Range, Lbs.	3410-3780
Wheelbases, Ins.	120
6 Cyl. Engines, BHP	80, 122

Long America's most popular make, Chevrolet made mostly right moves at the right times in the Fifties, and perfectly reflected that ebullient decade. It was right, for example, to build the Bel Air, which expanded from a single 1950 hardtop into the division's top-line series and went on to dominate Chevy production. It was also right to introduce the Corvette sports car and the equally legendary small-block V-8; both helped to banish Chevy's staid image forever. And it was right to add strength at the top of the line with the '58 Impala.

The last of the traditional low-cost, low-suds Chevys appeared for 1950-52, based on the successful, restyled 1949 models conceived under the direction of GM design chief Harley Earl. The 1950 line again divided between Fleetline two- and four-door fastback sedans and a group of notchback Styleline models, each offered in base Special and costlier DeLuxe trim; the latter accounted for some 80-85 percent of sales. Stylelines comprised two-door Town Sedan, sport coupe, and four-door Sport Sedan, plus a Special business coupe and a Deluxe-trim convertible and four-door all-steel wagon.

This basic array would persist through 1952 save the Fleetline Specials and DeLuxe four-door, which vanished after '51. By 1953, the surviving Fleetline DeLuxe two-door would be gone too.

These early-decade Chevys continued with the division's hoary Thirties-vintage "Stovebolt Six," which for 1950 was coaxed up to 92 horsepower for the 216.5-cubic-inch version (bore and stroke: 3.50 × 3.75 inches) used with manual transmission. But there was also a 235.5-cid unit (3.56 × 3.94 inches) with 105 bhp for cars equipped with optional two-speed Powerglide, Chevy's new fully automatic transmission. Powerglide, a torque-converter design similar to Buick's Dynaflow, was a big reason Chevy beat Ford in 1950 model-year car production by no less than 290,000 units.

Chevy also beat its rivals to the punch for 1950 with America's first low-priced hardtop coupe, the aptly named Bel Air. Like the pioneering Buick, Cadillac, and Olds hardtops of 1949, this junior edition was a top-line offering with lush trim that included simulated convertible-top bows on the headliner.

The division took a breather for 1951-52. There were no major mechanical developments, and styling changes were confined to somewhat bulkier sheetmetal for '51 and detail trim revisions for '52. Chevy remained Detroit's production leader in both years. The '51 totals were 1.23 million to runner-up Ford's 1.013 million. Korean War restrictions forced industry-wide cutbacks for '52, but Chevy's 800,000-plus still beat Ford's 671,000.

Though the Motorama-inspired Corvette sports car, detailed further on in this book, was Chevy's glamour news for '53, the all-important passenger models weren't forgotten, receiving a major facelift and new names. Specials were retitled One-Fifty, DeLuxes became Two-Tens, and Bel Air was applied to a convertible, hardtop Sport Coupe, and two sedans in a new top-line series. Two-Ten duplicated all but the convertible and added a long-deck club coupe and two four-door wagons: six-

1950 Chevrolet Styleline DeLuxe convertible coupe

1950 Chevrolet Styleline DeLuxe Bel Air hardtop coupe

1951 Chevrolet Styleline DeLuxe convertible coupe

1952 Chevrolet Styleline DeLuxe Bel Air hardtop coupe

passenger Handyman and three-seat eight-passenger Townsman (which would become a Bel Air for '54). The One-Fifty offered just the Handyman, plus two sedans, club coupe, and stripped business coupe.

Also for '53, Chevy dropped its smaller six and boosted compression on the 235 to create what was dubbed the "Blue Flame Six," rated at 105 bhp with manual shift or 115 with Powerglide. The figures were 115 and 125 for 1954, when styling became a bit flashier. Chevy continued to set the production pace. With war restrictions ended, volume soared to over 1.3 million units for '53 and was near 1.17 million for '54.

Without question, the new 265 Chevrolet V-8 of 1955 was one of Detroit's milestone engines. Though designed for efficiency and low unit cost, it was really one of those "blue sky" projects that comes along only once or twice in an engineer's career.

Ed Cole and Harry Barr had reason to be enthusiastic. The 265 had low reciprocating mass that allowed high rpm; die-cast heads with integral, interchangeable valve guides; aluminum "slipper" pistons; and a crankshaft of forged pressed-steel instead of alloy iron—and much more. Best of all, it weighed less than the old six yet was far more potent, initially pumping out 162/170 bhp manual/Powerglide or 180 bhp with optional Power-Pak (four-barrel carburetor and dual exhausts).

Of course, it could give a lot more—and did when bored out to 283 cid (3.88 × 3.00 inches) for 1957 and offered with optional fuel injection. Chevrolet developed a new 348-cid "big-block" V-8 for 1958 and beyond. Though the big-block was a good engine, the small-block remains the best-known, best-loved engine of its day, earning Chevy a performance reputation the way its sixes never could.

At just under $200, Powerglide was an increasingly popular option as the Fifties progressed: a smooth operator well suited to all but very high-powered Chevys. Standard three-speed manual and extra-cost stick-overdrive were offered throughout the decade, and an all-synchromesh four-speed manual came onstream in 1959. Late '57 brought a second automatic option, three-speed Turboglide, but it was complex, costly and short-lived.

Besides V-8 power, Chevy's 1955 passenger models sported sensational new styling that was probably even more a factor in record division sales in that banner industry year. Design principals Clare MacKichan, Chuck Stebbins, Bob Veryzer, and Carl Renner worked under Harley Earl's dictum of "Go all the way, then back off." Though the '55 didn't reach showrooms looking like it did in fanciful renderings, it wasn't far off, wearing Earl's hallmark beltline dip, wraparound windshield, and a simple eggcrate grille inspired by Ferrari.

Other elements in Chevy's winning '55 package included a more capable suspension, bigger brakes, better steering, more interior and trunk room, better visibility—the list was almost endless. Even the old six was improved, boosted to 123/136 bhp manual/Powerglide. With all this, plus attractive prices not changed much from '54 (mostly in the $1600-$2260 range), Chevy

1953 Chevrolet Bel Air four-door sedan

1953 Chevrolet Two-Ten DeLuxe convertible coupe

1953 Chevrolet Corvette roadster

convincingly won the production race with some 1.7 million cars, a quarter-million units better than Ford.

An interesting '55 newcomer was the Bel Air Nomad, America's first "hardtop wagon." A Carl Renner idea adapted for the passenger Chevy from a 1954 Motorama Corvette, the Nomad didn't sell all that well, mainly because two-door wagons were less popular than four-doors, though water leaks were also a problem. Then too, it was relatively expensive—$2600-$2700. Had anybody else built it, the Nomad would probably have seen minuscule production, but a respectable 8386 were built for 1955, 7886 for '56, and 6103 for 1957.

Chevy called its '55 "The Hot One." Ads said the '56 was even hotter. It was. The old six, now teaming with manual shift only, was up to 140 bhp; the V-8 delivered up to 225 bhp with Power-Pak (four-barrel carburetor and

1954 Chevrolet Bel Air Sport Coupe hardtop

1956 Chevrolet Bel Air convertible coupe

1955 Chevrolet Bel Air Sport Coupe hardtop

1956 Chevrolet Bel Air hardtop sedan

1955 Chevrolet Bel Air convertible coupe

1956 Chevrolet Corvette convertible coupe

dual exhausts). A $40 million restyle made all models look more like Cadillacs—especially the grille, which became broader, brighter, and more conventional in line with buyer tastes. Another GM innovation, four-door hardtops, joined the line as Two-Ten and Bel Air Sport Sedans. Despite a broad industry retreat, Chevy managed record market penetration of close to 28 percent on just 88 percent of its '55 volume—about 1.5 million units.

While Ford and Plymouth had all-new styling for '57, Chevy made do with another substantial facelift, though it was a fine one and quite popular. In fact, this Chevy has come to be regarded in some quarters as the definitive Fifties car. Engine choices now numbered seven, up two from '56, including no fewer than five 283 V-8s with 185 up to 283 bhp. The last came courtesy of "Ramjet" mechanical fuel injection, a new option that found few

takers among Chevy passenger-car buyers at $500 but enabled the division to claim "1 hp per cu. in." (though Chrysler had achieved that magic figure with its '56 300B). Yet the '57s were fast even without Ramjet. A Bel Air Sport Sedan with the four-barrel 270-bhp 283 would do 0-60 mph in 9.9 seconds, the quarter-mile in 17.5 seconds, and over 110 mph flat out.

Properly equipped, the 1955-57 Chevy was a formidable track competitor. Before the Automobile Manufacturers Association agreed to withdraw from organized racing in June 1957, Chevy did very well in NASCAR and other stock-car events. At that year's Daytona Speed Weeks, Chevy took the first three places in the two-way flying-mile for Class 4 (213-259 cid); in Class 5 (259-305 cid) it captured 33 of 37 events, the fastest car averaging 131.076 mpg. Chevy also won the 1957 Pure Oil Manufacturers

1957 Chevrolet Corvette convertible coupe

1957 Chevrolet Bel Air Nomad two-door station wagon

1957 Chevrolet Bel Air convertible coupe

1958 Chevrolet Corvette convertible coupe

Trophy with 574 points against 309 for runner-up Ford.

While the AMA "ban" didn't deter Chevy (and others) from providing under-the-table racing support, it was reflected in the 1958 models, and not everyone was pleased. Said *Mechanix Illustrated* magazine tester "Uncle" Tom McCahill: "When an ad man can't write about his product's success at Pikes Peak, Daytona Beach or Darlington, or how fast it gets away from a traffic light, what's he got left? All he can do is tell about the hand-woven Indian rugs on the floor, the Da Vinci sculptured door handles, or the '10 miles per gallon' it averaged under the featherfoot of a professional economy jockey."

McCahill was right. Riding a new X-member chassis with 117.5-inch-wheelbase (up 2.5 inches from 1949-57), the '58 Chevys were longer, lower, wider and heavier—though not really slower than the lighter and lively '57s. Leading the line was the lush new Impala, a Bel Air sub-series offering convertible and Sport Coupe hardtop with six or V-8 in the $2600-$2800 range. The division was now reaching for a buyer group it had never sought before: the solid, substantial Pontiac types who cared more about size and comfort than performance or handling. Impala delivered. Despite a rough year for Detroit and the U.S. economy as a whole, Chevy managed over 1.1 million cars, of which 60,000 were Impalas.

Chevy's '58 bodies were naturally all-new too—and shinier, more "important," and more Cadillac-like than ever. As it turned out, they were one-year-only jobs. Not so the new 348 big-block V-8, a modified truck design (which Chevy naturally failed to mention) offering 250 or 280 bhp. The standard V-8 was a lone 185-bhp 283, the standard six a 145-bhp Blue Flame.

Models below Impala were shuffled for '58. One-Fifty was now Delray (a name borrowed from a spiffy 1955-57 Two-Ten two-door sedan), Biscayne replaced Two-Ten, and "Station Wagon" was a separate series with no fewer than five models: two-door Yeoman and four-door Yeoman, Brookwood, and Nomad, with the last two seating six or nine. Unlike the 1955-57 original, the '58 Nomad was a conventional wagon.

Chevrolet deserved credit for deemphasizing tailfins for '58, but made up for it the next year with another all-new body that replaced the distinctive "gullwing" rear with huge cat's-eye taillamps and a batwing deck that Uncle Tom described as "big enough to land a Piper Cub."

Ford had shaded Chevy in '57-model production, and came within 12,000 units of doing so again for '59. Chevy's 1959 styling excesses no doubt played a part—and partly explains why the 1960 Chevys were a lot more subdued. Another reason was the advent of William L. Mitchell as GM design chief, who replaced Harley Earl on his 1958 retirement.

Delray disappeared from the '59 fleet, and a new top-line Impala series pushed everything else down a notch. All models rode a new 119-inch wheelbase, Chevy's longest ever. The growth between 1957 and 1959 was amazing: length up by nearly 11 inches, width by seven, weight by 300 pounds. The '59s were the first of the overstuffed "standard" Chevys that would endure for the next 15 years, though they made sense at the time. Buyers seemed to demand ever-bigger cars in the Fifties, so even the low-priced three grew to about the size of late-Forties Cadillacs and Lincolns. Chevy led in this area, too, and Ford and Plymouth were bound to follow.

They did not follow Chevy's Corvette into the narrow market realm of sports cars. Ford, however, was moved to reply with a more conventional and luxurious two-seater in the 1955 Thunderbird, which would prove a key factor in saving Corvette from an early grave. After that, it instantly matured into what Chevy rightly called "America's only true sports car."

Corvette debuted in January 1953 as a production-ready Motorama show car, culminating a 30-month development effort between Harley Earl's staff and Chevrolet Engineering. Enthusiastic public response prompted management to okay production of the two-seat roadster—a brave decision, as sales of import sports cars then amounted to less than one percent of the market. Production commenced June 30, 1953.

The Corvette's 102-inch wheelbase was identical with that of the Jaguar XK120, one of Earl's personal favorites, but its chassis was basically a cut-down Chevrolet passenger-car frame, though with numerous changes. Body construction was unique: the first use of fiberglass in a series-production car by a major manufacturer. Styling was unmistakable: rounded and rather bulbous, with "rocket" taillights, a toothy grille, and Earl's trendy wrapped windshield. If not exactly timeless, it looked great in '53.

Unfortunately, production problems and marketing miscues contributed to disappointing Corvette sales. Just 315 were built for '53 (most reserved for promotion and favored VIPs), followed by 3640 for '54 and a mere 674 of the '55s. Some observers lay the anemic sales at the doorstep of the car's odd mix of features. Boulevardier types disliked the plastic side curtains, clumsy cloth top, and lack of a back seat. Sports-car purists chided the gimmicky styling and plodding drivetrain, which for 1953-54 comprised only Powerglide and the ancient 235 "Stovebolt" six, though with triple carbs, high-lift cam, higher compression, and other tweaks that produced a commendable 150 bhp.

With sales paltry, GM management was ready to pull Corvette's plug in late 1954. Then came the Thunderbird, a competitive challenge that corporate pride couldn't ignore. Pleas from Earl and Chevy chief engineer Ed Cole also helped. And Cole had what would be the car's ultimate salvation: the brilliant 265 V-8 being readied for 1955 passenger Chevys. It was duly decreed for the sports car and tuned for 195 bhp, which vastly improved performance. As a result, all but six '55 Corvettes were so equipped. A three-speed floorshift manual gearbox, introduced as a late-season option, further aided performance and the shift of Corvette's image from "plastic bathtub" to serious sports car.

Corvette became very serious with the beautiful, all-new second generation of 1956. A rounded rump and sculptured bodysides with curving, concave sections just aft of the front wheel openings—an element seen on several recent Motorama showmobiles—contributed to a

1958 Chevrolet Bel Air Impala convertible coupe

1958 Chevrolet Delray two-door sedan

1959 Chevrolet Impala Sport Coupe hardtop

1959 Chevrolet Impala convertible coupe

1959 Chevrolet Corvette convertible coupe

stunning improvement over the stubby, slab-sided original. Proper roll-up door windows and an optional lift-off hardtop (both previewed on a 1954 Motorama Corvette) made motoring more civilized. Dropping the six and tuning the V-8 for 210 or 225 bhp (the latter via high-lift cam, twin four-barrel carbs, and dual exhausts) made performance truly thrilling, while handling became far more adept thanks to chassis changes wrought by recently hired engineer Zora Arkus-Duntov. The close-ratio manual three-speed became standard, shifting Powerglide to the options sheet. With all this, the most potent '56 Vette could hit 60 mph from rest in just 7.5 seconds and top 120 mph.

There was no need to change styling for '57, but Chevy upped performance by offering no fewer than five versions of its new 283 V-8, delivering 220 up to an amazing 283 bhp, the latter courtesy of Ramjet fuel injection. A four-speed manual transmission arrived in May at $188 extra, and combined with axle ratios as low as 4.11:1 to make "fuelie" '57s thunderingly fast. Published road tests showed 0-60 in 5.7 seconds, 0-100 mph in 16.8 seconds, the standing quarter-mile in 14.3 seconds at 96 mph, and a maximum 132 mph plus. However, Ramjet was no less costly or troublesome than in passenger Chevys, and 1957 installations amounted to only 240. Chevy also offered a new $725 "heavy-duty racing suspension" package with high-rate springs and shocks, front anti-roll bar, quick steering, and ceramic-metallic brake linings with finned ventilated drums. With one of the high-power engines, a Corvette was virtually ready to race right off the showroom floor.

Indeed, Corvette now began making its mark in competition. Dr. Richard Thompson won the national Sports Car Club of America C-Production championship in 1956, then took the '57 crown in B-Production, where the Vette qualified by dint of the larger V-8. John Fitch's '56 was the fastest modified car at that year's Daytona Speed Weeks, a Corvette finished 9th in the gruelling 12 Hours of Sebring in '56, and another came 2nd at Pebble Beach. Chevy's all-out 1957 assault on Sebring saw failure for the Vette-inspired Super Sport bubble-top experimental, but production models finished 1-2 in the GT class and a praiseworthy 12th and 15th overall.

Nineteen fifty-eight brought a busier, shinier Corvette that was 10 inches longer than its predecessors, more than two inches wider, and some 200 pounds heavier. The basic shape was broadly the same as 1956-57 except for quad headlamps (all the rage that year), a dummy air scoop ahead of each bodyside "cove," simulated hood louvers, and equally silly longitudinal chrome strips on the trunklid. Yet there were genuine improvements, including sturdier bumpers and a redesigned cockpit with a passenger grab bar, locking glovebox, and all instruments gathered right ahead of the driver. Despite the added heft and hokum, performance remained vivid because engines were little changed. The top fuel-injected 283 actually gained seven horsepower for 290 total, thus exceeding the hallowed "1 hp per cu.in." benchmark. Inflation plagued the national economy in '58 , yet Corvette's base price remained reasonable at $3631. Critics generally liked the '58. So did buyers. Model year production gained 2829 units over the '57 tally as Corvette turned a profit for the first time.

Volume rose another 500 units for '59, when Chevy smoothed out the hood, deleted the chrome trunk straps, and added trailing radius rods to counteract rear axle windup in hard acceleration, the year's main mechanical change. This basic package would continue for 1960, when production broke the magic 10,000-unit barrier.

Despite its move from pur sang sports car to plush GT, the third-generation Corvette was no less a track competitor than the second. Highlights include a GT-class win and 12th overall at Sebring '58, national SCCA B-Production crowns in 1958-59, fastest sports car at the 1958 Pikes Peak Hill Climb, and a slew of private victories. But it was sportsman Briggs Cunningham who gave America's sports car perhaps its finest racing hour, when one of his three team cars finished 8th in the 1960 running of the fabled 24 Hours of Le Mans.

As had Chevrolet itself. Within five short years the division had completely transformed its stock-in-trade from family haulers to hot haulers that were as big and plush as many costlier cars with more prestigious names. It was a dramatic turnaround for "USA-1," but a timely one that would prove a solid foundation for even greater success in the Sixties.

CHEVROLET AT A GLANCE										
Model Year	1950	1951	1952	1953	1954	1955	1956	1957	1958	1959
Price Range, $	1329-1994	1460-2191	1530-2297	1524-3513	1539-3523	1593-2934	1734-3149	1885-3465	2013-3631	2160-3875
Weight Range, Lbs.	3025-3460	3040-3470	3045-3475	2705-3495	2705-3540	2620-3385	2764-3516	2730-3566	2793-3839	2840-4020
Wheelbases, Ins.	115	115	115	102-115	102-115	102-115	102-115	102-115	102-117.5	102-119
6 Cyl. Engines, BHP	92-105	92-105	92-105	108-150	115-150	123-155	140	140	145	135
8 Cyl. Engines, BHP						162-195	162-225	162-283	185-280	185-315

Chrysler entered the Fifties as a high-volume make offering no fewer than seven series and 22 models. By 1959 it was an upper medium-price line with just 15 models in four series. Styling and engineering improved rapidly en route, the dowdy L-head cars of 1950 giving way to exciting, high-style performance machines by mid-decade. Chrysler also had some of the best-looking tailfins of the age.

Those fins, which arrived in grafted-on form for '55, were the work of Virgil M. Exner, who came to Chrysler from Studebaker in 1949. Exner liked "classic" elements: upright grilles, circular wheel openings, rakish silhouettes. What he found at Highland Park were the practical but boring engineering-oriented boxes favored by company president K.T. Keller (then preparing for retirement). Keller liked to say that "his" cars wouldn't knock your eyes out, but they wouldn't knock your hat off, either. Trouble was, people were turning away from upright practicality, and before Exner could get out any completely new cars, Chrysler Division's annual sales had fallen from 180,000 to barely 100,000.

The 1950 Chryslers were basically carryovers of the all-new 1949 models save a broad chrome eggcrate smile and the usual trim shuffles. Offerings started with low-priced Royal and step-up Windsor series powered by a plodding 250.6-cubic-inch L-head six making 116 horsepower; a 135-bhp 323.5-cid straight eight powered Saratoga, New Yorker, Imperial, and the long Crown Imperial. Royal and Saratoga rode 125.5-inch wheelbases, and each included a solitary long sedan on a 139.5-inch span. An in-between 131.5-inch spread was used by other models save Crown Imperials, which rode a 145.5-inch chassis. A Deluxe Imperial sedan with custom interior was new for 1950, but the big event that year was Chrysler's first volume hardtop coupe. Called Newport, it was available as a Windsor, New Yorker, and wood-trimmed Town & Country, that year's sole T&C model (replacing the 1946-49 ragtop).

Several models were on their way out in 1950. The six-cylinder Royals, selling for less than $2200, would not return for '51. Ditto the T&C, now with a pioneering four-wheel disc-brake system, but no longer needed to glamorize an unglamorous group of cars as it had in the early postwar years. After '51, Town & Country would grace only Chrysler station wagons (and is with us yet, though on a minivan). Saratoga, another peripheral seller, would depart after 1952, as would long Windsor sedans and the 1950-51 Windsor Traveler, a Deluxe-trim utility sedan (quite a contradiction, that). Standard and Deluxe Windsors and New Yorkers then carried on until 1955's "Hundred Million Dollar Look," when only Deluxe trim was offered, remaining long models were canceled, and Imperial spun off as a separate make (see "Imperial").

With one singular exception, Chryslers didn't change much from 1951 through '54. Wheelbases stayed the same throughout, as did basic styling, though a more conservative grille marked the '51s. The '52s were all but identical (the firm didn't even keep separate production figures). Taillights are the only way to tell them apart: the '52s had built-in backup lamps. The '53s gained slightly bulkier lower-body sheetmetal, more chrome, and one-piece windshields. The '54s were a little "brighter" still. Body and series assignments stood pat, too, though 1953-54 brought a new Custom Imperial line with sedan and limousine on a 133.5-inch wheelbase, plus a standard-length Newport.

The above-mentioned exception was the hemispherical-head V-8 of 1951, unquestionably Chrysler's greatest achievement of the decade. Chrysler styling may have been bland, but its engineering was still anything but, and the brilliant "Hemi" was simply the newest example. Still, the Chrysler six had been the dominant seller for years, so its complete disappearance after 1954 surprised some. But that was just part of a plan instigated by Keller's successor, Lester Lum "Tex" Colbert. Then too, the Hemi left fewer buyers for the six: close to 100,000 in 1950 but only some 45,000 by '54.

Colbert took over as company president in 1950 with several goals in mind. The main ones were decentralized divisional management, a total redesign for all model lines as soon as possible, and an ambitious program of plant expansion and financing. Giving the divisions freer rein meant that those close to retail sales would have more say in mapping policy.

The Hemi helped polish Chrysler's image in a big way, staid styling notwithstanding. First offered on the '51

1950 Chrysler Town and Country Newport hardtop coupe

1950 Chrysler Town and Country Newport hardtop coupe

1952 Chrysler New Yorker Newport hardtop coupe

1953 Chrysler Custom Imperial Town Limousine six-passenger sedan

1953 Chrysler New Yorker DeLuxe convertible coupe

1954 Chrysler New Yorker DeLuxe four-door sedan

Saratoga, New Yorker, and Imperial, it wasn't really a new idea, but it did have exceptional volumetric efficiency and delivered truly thrilling performance. Lower compression allowed Hemis to run on lower-octane fuel than most other postwar overhead-valve V-8s, yet produce far more power for a given displacement.

And the Hemi had plenty of power even in initial 331-cid form. An early demonstration engine recorded 352 bhp on the dynamometer after minor modifications to camshaft, carburetors, and exhaust. Drag racers would later extract up to 1000 bhp. But all Hemis were complex and costly to build, requiring twice as many rocker shafts,

pushrods, and rockers; heads were heavy too. They were thus phased out by 1959 in favor of more conventional "wedge-head" V-8s, though they would return in Chrysler's great mid-size muscle cars of the Sixties.

And of course, the Hemi made for some very hot Chryslers in the Fifties. By dint of its lighter Windsor chassis, the Hemi Saratoga was the fastest Chrysler up to 1955; even right off the showroom floor it could run 0-60 mph in as little as 10 seconds and close to 110 mph flat out. Bill Sterling's Saratoga won the stock class and finished third overall—behind a Ferrari—in the 1951 Mexican Road Race. Chryslers also did well as NASCAR

1955 Chrysler Windsor DeLuxe Nassau hardtop coupe

1955 Chrysler New Yorker DeLuxe four-door sedan

stockers, though they were eclipsed in 1952-54 by the remarkable Hudson Hornets. Briggs Cunningham began running his outstanding Chrysler-powered sports cars in European road races, taking his C-5R to third overall at Le Mans '53 at an average 104.14 mph (against 105.85 mph for the winning Jaguar C-Type). Then came the mighty 1955 Chrysler 300 packing a stock Hemi tuned for 300 bhp. It dominated NASCAR in 1955-56, and might have done so longer had the Automobile Manufacturers Association not agreed to deemphasize racing after 1957.

1955 Chrysler C-300 hardtop coupe

The 300 was part of the all-new Exner-styled '55 line that cost $100 million to develop, hence the "Hundred Million Look" advertising hype. But it was worth the expense, boosting division volume to over 150,000 units and bringing appearance up to par with performance at last. Evolved from the long Exner line of Ghia-bodied Chrysler show cars, the '55s were clean and aggressive-looking on a slightly longer 126-inch wheelbase. Windsor DeLuxe was treated to a new 301-cid Hemi with 188 bhp. New Yorker retained a 331 rated at 250 bhp.

The '56s looked even better—rare for a period facelift—and offered more power. Windsors moved up to a 331 engine with 225 bhp standard and 250 optional. New Yorker offered 280 bhp via a newly stroked 354-cid Hemi. A 300B followup to the previous C-300 used the same engine tweaked to 340 bhp; with a hot multi-carb option it delivered 355 bhp—making it the first Detroit V-8 to break the "1 hp per cu. in." barrier. Chevy would do the same for '57, only with fuel injection.

1956 Chrysler Windsor four-door sedan

Exner reached his design pinnacle with the '57 Chryslers: longer, lower, wider and sleeker, with modest grilles and graceful fins. They still look pretty good today. That year's 300C was breathtaking: big and powerful yet safe and controllable—and offered as a convertible for the first time. A unique trapezoidal grille helped it stand apart from other models.

Supplementing hardtop coupes for 1955-56 were the Windsor Nassau and New Yorker St. Regis, conservatively two-toned and boasting slightly ritzier interiors than standard Newports. Neither returned for '57, but the hastily conceived '56 Newport hardtop sedans would carry on well into the Sixties. Town & Country wagons, Windsor, and New Yorker now offered seating for up to nine via a novel rear-facing third seat.

1956 Chrysler New Yorker convertible coupe

Saratoga also returned for '57, and the revived mid-range series promptly sold over 37,000 copies. It again offered a performance premium in a 295-bhp 354-cid Hemi. That year's Windsors boasted 285 bhp. New Yorkers moved up to a stroked 392 with 325 bhp. In the 300C that engine was tuned for an incredible 375 or 390 bhp. In these years, nobody ran the "horsepower race" better than Chrysler.

PowerFlite two-speed automatic transmission had come along in 1954. For mid-'56 it was joined by three-speed TorqueFlite, one of the finest automatics ever built. That same year, Chrysler offered its now-famous (or infamous) pushbutton transmission controls, mounted in a handy pod to the left of the steering wheel.

Chrysler's 1957 styling was superb, but setting the pace

1957 Chrysler New Yorker hardtop sedan

made for sloppy workmanship and a tendency to early body rust (one reason relatively few of these cars survive today). A series of strikes hardly helped. Even so, Chrysler moved close to 125,000 cars for the model year, down from its 128,000 for '56, but still good enough for 10th in the industry.

No discussion of Chrysler in the Fifties is complete without a mention of "Torsion-Aire Ride," offered from 1957 on. Torsion bars weren't a new idea (Packard had introduced an excellent four-wheel system for '55), but Torsion-Aire went a long way toward proving big American cars could offer competent handling. Instead of sending road shocks up into the car as with coil or leaf springs, torsion bars absorbed most of them by twisting up against their anchor points. Chrysler used them only at the front—likely for more engine compartment space than improved suspension geometry—in conjunction with tuned leaf springs at the rear. Nevertheless, torsion bars must be regarded as a major step toward better handling.

A deep national recession and buyer dissatisfaction with assembly quality made 1958 a terrible year for Chrysler. Volume plunged to less than 64,000 units and the make dropped to 11th, still trailing Cadillac (as it had since '56). Styling stood mostly pat, but a convertible was added to the Windsor line, which was put on the 122-inch Dodge/DeSoto wheelbase. Horsepower kept climbing: Windsors were up to 290 bhp and Saratogas to 310 from 354-cid Hemis; New Yorkers packed 345 bhp and the latest 300D a smashing 380/390 from 392s.

A more substantial restyle marked the "lion-hearted" '59s. Though less graceful, they scored close to 70,000 sales in that year's recovering market. The switch to all-new wedgehead V-8s brought a 383-cid unit with 305 bhp for Windsor and 325 for Saratoga: a big-bore 413 gave 350 bhp in New Yorker and 380 bhp in the 300E. Though not as efficient as the Hemi, the wedge was much simpler and cheaper to build.

The 300E has been unduly criticized as a performance weakling against its Hemi-powered predecessors, but road tests said it was just as quick as a 300D. With 10.1:1 compression, TorqueFlite, and a 3.31:1 rear axle, the E could run 0-60 mph in less than 8.5 seconds and reach 90 mph in 17.5 seconds. Even so, production was just 550 hardtops and a mere 140 convertibles, a record low for the

1958 Chrysler New Yorker hardtop coupe

1959 Chrysler New Yorker convertible coupe

letter-series that would stand until 1963.

All told, Chrysler built some of its best cars in the Fifties, certainly some of its most exciting. For obvious reasons, the 300s became high-priced keepsakes years ago, but lesser post-'54 models have moved up in collector esteem—the well-built 1955-56s in particular—and prices seem likely to keep climbing. The cars are certainly worthy of that, and a hallowed place in the automotive hall of fame.

CHRYSLER AT A GLANCE										
Model Year	**1950**	**1951**	**1952**	**1953**	**1954**	**1955**	**1956**	**1957**	**1958**	**1959**
Price Range, $	2134-5384	2388-6740	2495-7044	2472-7044	2541-7044	2660-4209	2870-4419	3088-5359	3129-5603	3204-5749
Weight Range, Lbs.	3540-5305	3570-5450	3550-5430	3600-5275	3565-5295	3925-4430	3900-4460	3995-4490	3860-4475	3735-4360
Wheelbases, Ins.	125.5-145.5	125.5-145.5	125.5-145.5	125.5-145.5	125.5-145.5	126	126	126	122-126	122-126
6 Cyl. Engines, BHP	116	116	119	119	119					
8 Cyl. Engines, BHP	135	180	180	180	195-235	188-300	225-340	285-390	290-390	305-380

Clipper lived as a make distinct from Packard for but a single year, the year the "last real Packards" were made in Detroit before plummeting corporate fortunes prompted Studebaker-based replacements built at South Bend. But Clipper was intended to be far more, and therein lies a tale.

It began when marketing wizard James J. Nance was recruited from Hotpoint in 1952 to replace Hugh Ferry as president of a still-independent Packard. Blowing in like a tornado, Nance declared that the firm's continued emphasis on medium-price cars after World War II had been "bleeding the Packard name white." Accordingly, he grouped the 200/250-series into a Packard Clipper line for 1953, then registered Clipper as a separate make for '56, thus divorcing the cheaper models from the luxury Packards in both fact and name. There were even separate Clipper and Packard dealer signs in '56, and a Packard-Clipper Division of Studebaker-Packard Corporation (Packard had purchased debt-ridden Studebaker in 1954). "Packard" appeared nowhere on the cars except for tiny decklid script—and some didn't even have that.

Beyond that was S-P's expansive 1957 program that included Clippers on the larger of two all-new Studebaker platforms and Packards with larger new bodies all their own, plus visibly different appearance. But these plans were rendered stillborn when lenders refused to provide adequate funding as S-P continued to hemorrhage red ink. Predictably, Nance resigned (in August 1956, though soon resurfacing at the equally ill-starred new Edsel Division of Ford Motor Company).

Temporary salvation came by way of a management agreement with Curtiss-Wright Corporation, which used S-P mainly as a tax write-off. But with that, the '57 Packard was reconstituted as a deluxe Studebaker with slightly different—and rather more bizarre—styling. Called Packard Clipper, it ended the separate Clipper make. A year later, Packard itself was gone too.

The '56 Clipper line comprised five models: Deluxe, Super, and Custom four-door sedans and Super and Custom Constellation hardtop coupes. All shared a 122-inch wheelbase and an overhead-valve Packard V-8 of 352 cubic inches producing 275 horsepower for Customs, 240 bhp in other models. Also featured was Packard's innovative Torsion-Level suspension, continued from '55, although a conventional suspension was available on the bottom-line Deluxe. Options included overdrive manual transmission ($110), self-shift Ultramatic ($199), power steering, power brakes, and air conditioning.

These Clippers were luxuriously trimmed and nicely styled, though their sales volume wasn't sufficient to help floundering S-P. The Deluxe sedan was the bestseller, attracting 5715 buyers. The handsome Custom Constellation hardtop was rarest, accounting for fewer than 1500 units. As on senior Packards, styling was evolved from 1955's heavy facelift on John Rinehart's 1951 "high pockets" bodyshell, deftly executed by Richard A. Teague. Though still obvious Packard relatives, the Clippers retained their own grille and taillamp designs, made even more different for '56.

1956 Clipper Super hardtop coupe

1956 Clipper Custom Constellation hardtop coupe

Making Clipper a separate make was a good idea that came too late. Had the firm taken this approach in the huge seller's market of 1946, Packard might well be with us today.

CLIPPER AT A GLANCE				
Model Year	1950	1951	1952	1956
Price Range, $				2731-3164
Weight Range, Lbs.				3745-3860
Wheelbases, Ins.				122
8 Cyl. Engines, BHP				240-275

Officially, the Continental "Marks" of 1956-58 were not Lincolns but products of a separate Ford division created to establish Dearborn's dominance at the very top of the market—even above Cadillac. Only one model was offered for 1956-57: the flawlessly styled, beautifully crafted Mark II, priced at a stratospheric $10,000, but worth every penny. Yet Ford lost about $1000 on every one, because this was primarily an "image" car—more ego trip than calculated profit-maker. Ford then attempted to put Continental in the black with a lower-priced 1958-60 line based on the giant "unibody" Lincoln of those years, but it never sold particularly well.

Dealers and customers had pleaded with Ford to revive the Lincoln Continental since the last of the original line in 1948. But there was no money until 1953, when profits were looking up and Dearborn managers, determined to outflank rival GM in every market sector, approved a development program to recreate the Continental in the contemporary idiom.

William Clay Ford, younger brother of company president Henry Ford II, was put in charge of a new Special Products Division to come up with a design. After calling in five outside consultants to submit their ideas for comparison, management reviewed 13 different proposals and unanimously selected the one from...Special Products.

1956 Continental Mark II hardtop coupe

1957 Continental Mark II hardtop coupe

1958 Continental Mark III convertible coupe

1958 Continental Mark III convertible coupe

1959 Lincoln Continental Mark IV Landau hardtop sedan

It was, nevertheless, an excellent choice. Harley F. Copp, the division's chief engineer, gave it a unique "cowbelly" chassis dipped low between front and rear axles to permit high seating without a high roofline. The cabin was thus roomy, as well as starkly simple but also richly appointed in the fine broadcloth and nylon or Scottish Bridge of Weir leather. The dash echoed locomotive and aircraft design with full instrumentation and large toggle controls.

Chosen power was the 368-cubic-inch V-8 destined for the all-new '56 Lincolns, with the same 285 horsepower. However, Mark II units would be specially selected from the assembly line and individually adjusted before installation. The same applied to the transmission, Lincoln's three-speed Turbo-Drive automatic, also new for '56, and the 3.07:1 rear axle.

Actually, pains were taken all over the Mark II at a special "go-slow" plant. Bodies, for instance, were first trial-fitted to chassis, then painted, sanded, and polished by hand. Chrome plating exceeded industry standards. Nuts and bolts were torqued by people, not machines. Finally, before shipment, each car was given a 12-mile road test, followed by a detailed inspection and correction of any defects.

Appearing on a 126-inch wheelbase, the sleek and timeless Mark II measured 218.5 inches overall and weighed close to 4900 pounds. It came only as hardtop coupe, though a retractable hardtop-convertible had been envisioned (an idea later evolved by Ford Division into the 1957-59 Skyliner). The price may have been breathtaking, but it reflected not only an unusual amount of hand labor but high luxury content. Indeed, air conditioning was the only option ($740); everything else was standard, including full power accessories.

The Mark II was greeted with great enthusiasm on both sides of the Atlantic, immediately hailed as a design landmark. But the euphoria didn't last. Continental Division hoped to add a beautiful four-door sedan and a convertible for 1958, but both these "line extensions" were doomed along with the hardtop coupe by results from the sales department (though not before a couple of convertible prototypes were built in 1957.) The Mark II was having little impact on the luxury market; General Motors was still the leader. Though a moneyed few were buying, the Mark II wasn't convincing those with slightly less cash to buy Lincolns. As a result, production totaled just 1325 of the '56s and a mere 444 of the near-identical '57 models.

Years later, one Ford executive declared the Mark II program, on balance, a big mistake. "For obvious reasons we don't like to talk about it...What we had going for us in the Mark II was literally a revival of the Duesenberg concept. What we ended up with was something much less—and even that didn't last long...It was a project that for a time broke Bill Ford's heart, and I guess you could say that in many ways it broke ours too."

In line with an upper-management decision, price was cut drastically for 1958's "new" Continental, the Mark III. The result of recommendations from a Mercury cost

1959 Lincoln Continental Mark IV Landau hardtop sedan

analyst, this square-rigged Lincoln-based leviathan had a 131-inch wheelbase, elongated fenders, large chrome appliques, canted quad headlamps, a reverse-slant roofline, and a huge new 430-cid V-8 with 375 bhp. Convertible, four-door sedan, hardtop coupe, and Landau hardtop sedan were offered in the $5800-$6200 range. All sported a unique rear window that dropped down electrically for flow-through interior ventilation. Standard luxuries abounded once more, but not hand crafts-manship. The Mark III was "built to a price," and that helped improve sales, which totaled 12,550—respectable for that difficult, recessionary model year.

But the luxury market had shriveled badly, so Ford canceled Continental as a separate marque after 1958, though a little-changed Mark III returned in the Lincoln line as the 1959 Mark IV (see "Lincoln"). Continental Division was folded into Lincoln-Mercury, which also absorbed fast-faltering Edsel Division, thus ending Ford's mid-Fifties dream of a GM-style five-division structure.

A decade later came a new Mark III, so numbered to signal its "official" status as the Mark II's lineal successor. This was never anything but a Lincoln, however. Also unlike its forebear, it was an immediate sales success.

But though the Mark II failed commercially, it remains not only one of America's most memorable Fifties automobiles but one of the all-time design greats—a triumph of elegance and restraint in an era when Detroit produced precious little of either. The '58 Mark III offered proof of that lack, though it wasn't nearly as bad as it's often portrayed. Perhaps its greatest problem was having to follow the Mark II, which would have been difficult even in the best of times.

CONTINENTAL AT A GLANCE				
Model Year	**1956**	**1957**	**1958**	**1959**
Price Range, $	9695	9966	5825-6283	6598-10,230
Weight Range, Lbs.	4825	4800	4865-5040	4967-6000
Wheelbases, Ins.	126	126	131	131
8 Cyl. Engines, BHP	285	300	375	350

CROSLEY

A dolf Hitler launched his "people's car" in 1939. That same year, Powel Crosley, Jr., American tycoon of radios and refrigerators, launched his own *volkswagen:* an economy runabout with a tiny 80-inch wheelbase, 39.8-cubic-inch air-cooled twin, and the lowest price in the land: $325-$350. Measuring just 10 feet long and weighing a bit under half a ton, the Crosley packed a mighty 13.5 horsepower and could do no more than 50 mph (the factory recommended cruising at 40), but could return at least 50 miles per gallon. Sales were predictably handled through stores that carried Crosley's appliances.

Trouble was, Americans weren't interested in buying cars that way, let alone minimal cars of this type, so sales totaled a modest 2017 in 1939. Volume fell to just 422 of the little-changed 1940 models, then picked up to about 5000 for the stronger, more durable 1941-42 offerings of standard and DeLuxe convertible sedans, wood-body station wagon, convertible, a "covered wagon" with full canvas top, plus commercial models.

For a wartime U.S. Navy project, Crosley developed an overhead-cam four-cylinder engine using brazed copper and sheet steel for the block. Called "CoBra," it was selected to power Crosley's first postwar cars. This five-main-bearing unit proved fairly successful in machinery from truck refrigerators to Mooney Mite airplanes, but was far less happy in a car. The copper-steel block was prone to electrolysis that caused holes to develop in the cylinders, thus necessitating early rebuilds. Seeking to rectify matters, Crosley rushed out a cast-iron version—called CIBA, for Cast-Iron Block Assembly—of the same 44-cubic-inch size (bore and stroke: 2.50 × 2.25 inches) and 26.5 bhp. Significantly, price guides of the day listed higher trade-in values for the cast-iron engine, including retrofitted 1946-48 models.

Production of the '46 Crosleys began in June. A two-door four-seat sedan appeared first, followed later in the year by a convertible. A wagon returned for '47, the delivery sedan for '48. Commercial bodies also returned. Wheelbase was unchanged from that of prewar Crosleys, but styling endeavored to make the cars seem more "grown up"—which they were: 28 inches longer overall. Prices were more than double those of 1939. Still, at $888 in 1947, a Crosley was quite inexpensive.

For a time, things went well. Crosley built almost 5000 of its '46s, more than 19,000 for '47, and close to 29,000 of the '48s. Although Powel Crosley grandly predicted reaching 80,000 per year in the near future, his firm would never do so well again. New postwar designs from the independents and the Big Three, plus Crosley's reputation for engine problems, drastically depressed 1949 demand, and sales tumbled below 7500.

This was ironic, because the Crosley had become much better for '49. There was new styling with a smooth hood and integral front fenders, plus remote-control door handles and turn indicators on sedans and convertibles. In addition, Crosley fielded a smart little "bugeye" roadster called the Hotshot on an 85-inch wheelbase, priced at just $849.

Seeking to turn things around, Crosley offered wagon,

1950 Crosley Super Sports roadster

convertible, and sedan body styles in standard and Super trim for 1950, plus two roadsters: the doorless Hotshot and the slightly better-trimmed Super Sports, a Hotshot with conventional doors. Crosley was still in a class by itself on price—$872-$984 that year—but its engineering was also unique. Disc brakes, for example, had arrived for 1949-50, a first for series production shared with Chrysler's 1950 Town & Country Newport. Alas, insufficient development led the Crosley brakes to deteriorate quickly when exposed to road salt and grime, causing tremendous service woes. Since the firm was still smarting from the problems with its unlamented sheetmetal engine, this new headache was the last thing dealers (or customers) needed. Conventional drum brakes were reinstituted for '51.

Though the little roadsters failed to sell, they were tremendous class competitors on the track. A stock Hotshot or Super Sport could do up to 90 mph, and handling was excellent, thanks to a crude but effective semi-elliptic-and-coil-spring front suspension and quarter-elliptic rear suspension. The Hotshot's greatest accomplishment was winning the Index of Performance at Sebring in 1951 after a fine showing in the 12-hour endurance race.

But buyers were unmoved by this or anything else Crosley did (including the novel "Farm-O-Road" multi-purpose vehicle, a sort of pint-size Jeep-cum-farm tractor). Sales continued sliding: down to 6792 for 1950, then to 6614 for '51. The total was only 2075 for 1952 when the firm finally gave up on vehicles in July. It was soon acquired by General Tire and Rubber, which quickly disposed of its automotive operations after Powel Crosley had spent about $3 million trying to save them.

CROSLEY AT A GLANCE			
Model Year	**1950**	**1951**	**1952**
Price Range, $	882-984	943-1077	943-1077
Weight Range, Lbs.	1175-1403	1184-1403	1175-1403
Wheelbases, Ins.	80, 85	80, 85	80, 85
4 Cyl. Engines, BHP	26.5	26.5	26.5

DESOTO

Born in 1928, DeSoto was one of Detroit's few pre-Depression "expansion" makes to survive the Thirties, this despite the radical mid-decade Airflow that nearly proved fatal to the company's fortunes. DeSoto went on to build its most exciting cars in the Fifties, only to die in late 1960 after a flash recession and sibling rivalry obliterated its narrow, well-defined price niche. In between, DeSoto did good and occasionally great business as the medium-price "bridge" make between Dodge and Chrysler, with design and engineering that usually owed more to the latter than the former.

Reflecting Chrysler Corporation's overall retreat from innovation after the Airflow debacle, the DeSotos built through 1951 were solid but stolid cars powered by a tough but plodding L-head six. That engine, an Airflow legacy, was sized at 236.6 cubic inches (bore × stroke: 3.44 × 3.25 inches) and put out 109 horsepower from 1942 through March 1949, when DeSoto introduced its first postwar-design models and bumped rated power to 112. Styling predictably followed the pattern of other '49 Chrysler makes: the high-built, relatively compact "box" favored by company president K.T. Keller.

The '49 DeSotos returned for 1950 with somewhat sleeker rear ends and a newly divided grille bearing the make's then-familiar big chrome "teeth." Also returning was a hood mascot formed as a bust of explorer Hernando DeSoto; like many such ornaments of the time, it glowed when the parking or head lights were switched on.

Models, as usual, divided between base DeLuxe and uplevel Custom. All retained 1949's new 125.5-inch wheelbase (up four inches from 1941-48) save an eight-passenger sedan in each series and the unique Custom Suburban, all on a 139.5-inch span. Chrysler's Fluid Drive semi-automatic transmission with what DeSoto called "Tip-Toe Shift" became standard on Customs and a $121 option for DeLuxes.

Both series also included a club coupe and four-door sedan. Custom added a convertible, four-door wagon and—new for 1950—the $2489 Sportsman, DeSoto's first hardtop coupe. The Custom Suburban again boasted vast cargo room, standard roof-top luggage rack, and rear jump seats that made it a true nine-seater. Also putting in another appearance was a counterpart DeLuxe called "Carry-All," offering similar utility on the standard wheelbase. The Carry-All sold a respectable 3900 copies for 1950, but the Suburban managed just 623, though that bettered the previous year's 129; still, both utility sedans would depart after 1952. Wagons, which went from structural-wood to all-steel construction during 1950, sold poorly at just 600 and 100, respectively; they would not disappear, however, as rising wagon demand was a Fifties phenomenon throughout the industry.

Nineteen forty-nine was a spectacular year for most of Detroit, but not DeSoto. Volume remained at the '48 level—about 94,300—and the make dropped from 14th to 12th on the production roster. However, Customs outsold DeLuxes by 3-1, a sign of growing buyer preference for more luxurious cars. The pattern held for 1950, but output that model year leaped almost 45 percent to nearly

1950 DeSoto Custom Sportsman hardtop coupe

1951 DeSoto Custom four-door sedan

134,000, this despite relatively little change.

The '51s looked a bit sleeker thanks to the efforts of Virgil Exner, recently arrived from Studebaker to head Chrysler Corporation styling. DeSoto's old six was stroked to 250.6 cid (3.44 × 4.50), its largest size ever and good for 116 bhp. With government-ordered production cutbacks in force for the Korean War, DeSoto volume eased to 106,000, pushing the make from 12th down to 15th behind Kaiser (with its beautiful new '51 design) and Hudson (with its powerful new six-cylinder Hornets).

DeSoto's first-ever V-8 was the major development for '52. Called FireDome, it was a slightly smaller, 276.1-cid version (3.63 × 3.34) of the brilliant overhead-valve, hemispherical-head Chrysler unit introduced the previous year. With a rated 160 bhp, it put DeSoto firmly in Detroit's escalating "horsepower race."

The FireDome powered a new like-named top-line series that duplicated Custom offerings save the Suburban. It immediately garnered nearly 50,000 sales, but DeSoto could do no better than 88,000 total for the model year, though it moved up a bit in the production stakes, finishing 13th. The glowing Hernando hood mascot disappeared in favor of a scoop-like ornament.

For 1953, remaining Custom/DeLuxe models were combined into a new Powermaster Six series that still lagged behind the FireDome in sales, this time by 2-1. Both groups included Sportsman hardtops, and Exner's growing influence was seen in an update of the more massive 1951-52 look, highlighted by new one-piece windshields and more liberal brightwork. Model-year production jumped back to 130,000, moving DeSoto up to 11th place, its highest finish in years.

1953 DeSoto Firedome convertible coupe

1954 DeSoto Firedome four-door sedan

1955 DeSoto Fireflite Sportsman hardtop coupe

1955 DeSoto Fireflite Coronado four-door sedan

1956 DeSoto Fireflite Adventurer hardtop coupe

Adding much-needed pizzazz to DeSoto's dour image in '54 was the interesting Adventurer I show car, one in a series of sporty Exner designs begun with the 1951 Chrysler K-310. All were built by Ghia in Italy. Riding a shortened 111-inch wheelbase, Adventurer I was a close-coupled coupe sporting outside exhausts, wire wheels, and full instrumentation. Intriguingly, it almost made production. "Had it been mass-produced," Exner later said, "it would have been the first four-passenger sports car made in this country. It was better than a 2+2, and of course it had the DeSoto Hemi. It was my favorite car." Adventurer II followed in '55, a standard-chassis four-seat coupe designed more by Ghia than Exner. Painted deep red and lacking bumpers, it was sleek, but not quite as well proportioned as Adventurer I, and wasn't seriously considered for showroom sale.

Meantime, the first of Exner's new "Forward Look" production models was due for 1955, so DeSoto's old '49 bodyshell was modestly reworked one last time for '54. The V-8 was tweaked to 170 bhp, but the big news came at midyear with the debut of two-speed PowerFlite, Chrysler's first fully automatic transmission. This would be a DeSoto standard after '54, thus ending the standard three-speed manual. Fluid Drive was still around (at $130 extra), as was overdrive ($96). This would also be the last year for the long FireDome/Powermaster sedans—and the Powermaster itself. Reflecting Chrysler Corporation's 1954 sales nightmare, DeSoto model-year output tumbled to 76,580, and the make slipped to 12th.

Bolder, fully up-to-date new Exner styling and more powerful engines stood to turn things around for 1955. Firedome now played "second banana" to a new uplevel Fireflite line, though both rode a 126-inch wheelbase and had a Hemi V-8 bored out to 291 cid (3.72 × 3.44). Respective power ratings were 185 and 200. No '55 Chrysler product was sedate, but DeSoto was possibly the shiniest of all—though still attractive, with a much lower silhouette, wrapped windshield, the ever-toothy front end (though this would be the last), "gullwing" dash, and broad, optional two-toning. This package greatly appealed to buyers, boosting division output to nearly 115,000 units. Still, that was only good for 13th in a year when most every Detroit make did very well.

Firedome offered DeSoto's only '55 wagon, along with a detrimmed $2541 Special hardtop priced some $110 below its Sportsman counterpart. The plush Coronado sedan, a mid-1954 addition to the FireDome line, returned as a 1955 "spring special" Fireflite at $100 above the regular $2800 sedan. It's now a minor collector's item, mainly for having one of the industry's first three-tone paint jobs (turquoise, black, and white). Convertibles were available in both '55 DeSoto series but saw minuscule sales: just 625 FireDomes and 775 Fireflites.

For 1956, a longer stroke brought DeSoto's Hemi to 330.4 cid (3.72 × 3.80), lifting FireDome horsepower to 230 and Fireflite's to 255. The trademark grille teeth were replaced by fine mesh, and unreadable gold-on-white instruments appeared. But the big change, as on other Chrysler lines, was tailfins (still pretty modest) carrying

1956 DeSoto Fireflite Sportsman hardtop coupe

1957 DeSoto Adventurer hardtop coupe

distinctive "tri-tower" lamps—stacked pairs of round red lenses separated by a matching backup light.

Following GM's lead, four-door hardtops arrived in force: a Sportsman in each series and a lower-priced Firedome Seville. A Seville hardtop coupe replaced the previous Firedome Special. (Cadillac's new-for-'56 Eldorado two-door hardtop was also called Seville, but no legal battles ensued.) A mid-season highlight was the limited-edition Adventurer hardtop coupe, a supercar awash in gold-anodized aluminum trim. Carrying a new 320-bhp 341 Hemi (3.78 × 3.80), it was part of an expanded Highland Park performance squadron that included the Chrysler 300B, Plymouth Fury, and Dodge D-500. DeSoto paced that year's Indy 500, and the make celebrated by making about 100 "Pacesetter" convertibles: Fireflites with Adventurer-style trim, priced at $3615 apiece.

DeSoto shared in Detroit's overall '56 retreat, building about 4300 fewer cars; however, it returned to 11th place due to fast-fading sales at Nash and Hudson, Studebaker, and Packard. The division finished in that spot again for '57 even though volume jumped to about 110,500—as near as DeSoto ever came to passing Chrysler (ending up about 7200 units behind).

No wonder. For 1957, DeSoto was not only all-new for the second time in three years, but superbly engineered and strikingly styled. A low-cost Dodge-based Firesweep series on a 122-inch wheelbase joined Firedome and Fireflite (still on 126-inch chassis) in another effort to extend DeSoto's market territory. It helped. The Firesweep sedan sold for only $2777, where the cheapest Firedome cost $2958. The line also included two- and four Sportsman hardtops and two four-door wagons: six-seat Shopper and nine-passenger Explorer. That year's Fireflite series offered all those body styles plus a convertible; Firedome was the same, but had no wagons.

All were big, heavy, and powerful. The two upper series used 341 Hemis with 270 and 290 bhp, respectively. Firesweeps had the previous year's 330 debored to 325 cid (3.69 × 3.80) and tuned for 245 bhp standard or 260 bhp with optional four-barrel carburetor. Last but not least, a soft-top Adventurer joined the hardtop coupe to form a new limited-edition series above Fireflite, boasting 345 bhp from a twin-four-barrel Hemi modestly bored to 345 cid and exactly "square" dimensions (3.80 × 3.80).

Dramatic new Exner styling made finned fantasies of all

'57 Chrysler products. DeSoto's version of this second-generation Forward Look was quite handsome: dart-like profile, tri-tower taillamps attractively integrated into the soaring rear fenders, simple but pleasant side moldings, a unique front bumper/grille, acres more glass. DeSoto also benefited from Chrysler's 1957 corporate-wide switch to torsion-bar front suspension, which made these heavy-weights uncannily good handlers. Aiding performance was the arrival of quick, responsive three-speed TorqueFlite automatic transmission as an optional alternative to PowerFlite. Also controlled by Highland Park's oh-so-modern pushbuttons, it was a great automatic that would outlive DeSoto.

Yet as exciting as all this was, 1957 would prove DeSoto's last good year. Production plunged to 50,000 for '58, the make's lowest total in 20 years. The '58 recession, poor workmanship after '56, and unwise marketing decisions all contributed to a downward spiral from which DeSoto would never recover.

The '58 DeSotos were predictably much like the '57s save busier grilles, more ornate trim, and standard quad headlights. (Because some states had not approved "quadrilights" for '57, DeSoto front fenders were designed to accept either one or two lamps each, the latter available where law permitted. By '58, four-lamp systems were legal nationwide.) The '57 lineup returned, bolstered by a new Firesweep convertible. That year's Adventurer ragtop was the most expensive DeSoto ever ($4272), though Chrysler's corresponding 300D convertible cost $1300 more.

Engines and power ratings grew, but the Hemi was ever complicated and costly to build, so Chrysler began switching to cheaper wedgehead designs for '58. Among them were two DeSoto "Turboflash" V-8s. Firesweeps had a 350-cid edition (4.06 × 3.38) with 280 bhp standard or 295 with optional four-barrel carb. Other models used a big-bore 361 (4.13 × 3.38) packing 295 bhp in standard Firedome tune, 305 with twin four-barrels in Fireflites (optional on Firedomes), 345 in high-compression Adventurer guise, and a smashing 355 for Adventurers with optional Bendix fuel injection, which was expensive and thus rarely ordered.

Even without Hemi heads, the '58s DeSotos were quite quick, helped by fast-shifting TorqueFlite, now standard on Fireflites and Adventurers. (Firesweeps again had

1958 DeSoto Firesweep convertible coupe

1959 DeSoto Adventurer hardtop coupe

Adventurer. The last saw slightly improved sales, but total model-year production of just under 46,000 was hardly the sort that had sustained DeSoto earlier in the decade.

Rumors of DeSoto's imminent demise began cropping up in '59, and naturally affected sales. Though calendar-year output was up slightly from '58, volume for both years was less than half that of 1957's near 120,000 units. Plainly, the recession had put DeSoto in the same kind of trouble as Oldsmobile, Buick, and Mercury, but those makes started at higher levels and thus had further to fall. Moreover, all were planning smaller models for 1960-61. Although DeSoto's 1962 plans included "downsized" standard cars, there was no program for a compact.

But the real problem was a change in corporate marketing strategy. Previously, company franchises split into Chrysler-Plymouth, DeSoto-Plymouth, and Dodge-Plymouth dealers. The advent of Imperial as a separate make for 1955 prompted Chrysler Division to expand in the lower end of its market, while Dodge moved upward with larger and more luxurious cars. DeSoto had nowhere to go—except the grave.

At first, Chrysler strongly denied that DeSoto would be terminated, and even staged a 1959 celebration marking production of the two-millionth DeSoto. Press releases noted that almost a million DeSotos were still registered, and the division announced that $25 million had been earmarked for future models—$7 million for 1960 alone. Officials said commitments had been made for '61 too, and that work was underway toward 1962-63. They also pointed out that Chrysler had regularly made a profit on DeSoto.

But then Chrysler combined DeSoto and Plymouth Divisions in 1960, with the new compact Valiant an ostensibly separate make. Valiant sold very well and Plymouth did fairly well, but DeSoto fared poorly. Sales during the first two months of 1960 were just 4746 units—a mere 0.51 percent of the industry—down greatly from the 1959 period (6134 units and 0.72 percent).

Thus, by Christmas 1960, DeSoto's restyled '62s were shelved and production of the '61 models, announced that October, was halted. Some DeSoto-Plymouth dealers then became Chrysler-Plymouth stores—to the chagrin of existing C-P agents nearby. It was a sad finish for a once-proud make.

standard three-speed manual and offered the Firedome's standard PowerFlite at extra cost.) DeSotos remained some of the most roadworthy of Detroiters—and among the fastest. A Firedome with the 305-bhp setup could scale 0-60 mph in 7.7 seconds, 0-80 mph in 13.5 seconds, and reach 115 mph with little strain.

DeSoto claimed its towering tailfins of this era "added stability at speed," but it was pure propaganda. The fins did little from an aerodynamic standpoint under 80 mph. Their main purpose was to make Chrysler products stand out from the opposition, which they most definitely did.

But fins and flash couldn't keep DeSoto from being squeezed out of its market by Dodge from below and Chrysler from above, and though the same broad lineup returned for another year, 1959 marked the beginning of DeSoto's end. Firesweeps were upgraded to the 361 wedge, offered in just one, 295-bhp version. Other models got an even bigger-bore new 383 (4.25 × 3.38) with 305 bhp for Firedome, 325 for Fireflite, and 350 bhp for

DESOTO AT A GLANCE										
Model Year	**1950**	**1951**	**1952**	**1953**	**1954**	**1955**	**1956**	**1957**	**1958**	**1959**
Price Range, $	1996-3199	2235-3586	2339-3754	2364-3559	2364-3559	2498-3151	2678-3728	2777-4272	2819-4369	2904-4749
Weight Range, Lbs.	3450-4400	3475-4395	3435-4370	3480-4270	3505-4305	3805-4115	3780-4070	3645-4290	3660-4295	3625-4170
Wheelbases, Ins.	125.5, 139.5	125.5, 139.5	125.5, 139.5	125.5, 139.5	125.5, 139.5	126	126	122, 126	122, 126	122, 126
6 Cyl. Engines, BHP	112	116	116	116	116					
8 Cyl. Engines, BHP			160	160	170	188, 200	230-320	245-345	280-355	295-350

Chrysler Corporation transformed itself in the Fifties, abandoning stodgy, square-lined practicality for fins, flash, and fire. Actually, there was no choice. By 1954, too many years of too little change had Chrysler on the brink and Ford back at the number-two spot in industry sales. Though Chrysler wasn't in such dire straits as Studebaker or soon-to-be-extinct Kaiser-Willys, it was far from healthy. But it promptly got in back in the pink with bigger, bolder cars that often led the style and performance parade, instead of just following along.

Dodge, a part of the Chrysler family since 1928, naturally benefited from this product revolution, exchanging its "good old reliable" reputation for a "hot car" image that persists to this day. In this, the Dodge story of the Fifties parallels Chevrolet's, except that sales were more erratic.

Like most Detroit makes, Chrysler Corporation issued its first all-postwar designs for 1949, with high, slab-sided "three-box" styling (one box on two others) and familiar, pedestrian powerplants. Dodge was no different, and it again hewed to this company line for 1950 save smoother, more "important" looks.

Models again started with low-priced Wayfarers pitched just above the more expensive Plymouths: long-deck business coupe, fastback two-door sedan, and a unique two-seat roadster on Plymouth's 115-inch wheelbase. The roadster was named Sportabout for 1950—and was technically a convertible, as roll-up side windows were added. Price was still attractive at $1727, but the Sportabout attracted over 46 percent fewer sales than its '49 predecessor (2903 vs. 5420).

One step up were "standard" Dodges on a 123.5-inch platform: four-door sedans in Meadowbrook and nicer Coronet trim, plus Coronet club coupe (two-door sedan), convertible, and four-door wagon. The last was switched during the year from part-wood to all-steel construction, and gained the Sierra name with it. A 1950 newcomer was the Coronet Diplomat, putting Dodge into the fast-growing hardtop business started by GM the year before. As in recent years, Dodge also offered a seven-seat sedan on a 137.5-inch chassis; it would continue through 1952 for the taxi and limousine trades.

There's not much to say about Dodge styling through '52; it was uniformly dull. The same applies to motive power: a sturdy 230.2 cubic-inch flathead six (bore and stroke: 3.25 × 4.63 inches) with an unexciting 103 horsepower. Though it dated from the Thirties, it would serve Dodge through the end of this decade, by which time engineers had tweaked it to 138 bhp.

Despite ho-hum cars, Dodge did well in the early Fifties. Production was near 342,000 for 1950 and 290,000 for '51, good for seventh in the industry. Dodge maintained that rank with only 206,000 cars for '52 and a more satisfying 320,000 for '53, then dropped to eighth for '54 on volume of only 154,000.

Styling became a tad sleeker for 1951-52. Wheelbases were unchanged, but a lower grille opening, clean flanks, and faired-in taillights improved appearance. The most visible '52 alteration was paint applied to the grille bar just above the bumper.

1950 Dodge Coronet four-door sedan

1951 Dodge Wayfarer two-door sedan

A revised 1953 lineup included a lone Meadowbrook Suburban wagon and other two-door models on the 114-inch Plymouth wheelbase—thus reviving a stubby look; a 119-inch chassis supported six-cylinder Meadowbrook, Meadowbrook Special and Coronet sedans, and club coupes. But windshields were now one-piece, rooflines restyled, and trim moved around, all of which helped relieve what were still pretty slab-sided cars. As with all '53 Chrysler Corporation cars, this Dodge facelift marked the first direct influence of Virgil Exner, who'd come to Highland Park from Studebaker to be chief stylist a few years before.

But the big news for '53 was the Coronet Eight, a new top-line group of long-chassis club coupe and sedan and "shorty" convertible, Diplomat hardtop, and two-door Sierra powered by Dodge's first-ever performance engine: the brilliant Red Ram V-8. Arriving at 241.3 cid (3.44 × 3.25 inches), it delivered 140 bhp, but was capable of much more. In essence, it was a scaled-down version of 1951's new 331-cid Chrysler Hemi. Chrysler had long experimented with hemispherical combustion chambers and was now cashing in on the experience. Against other V-8s, the Hemi offered inherent advantages like smoother porting and manifold passages, larger valves set farther apart, better thermal efficiency, ample water jacketing, a nearly central sparkplug location, and low heat rejection into coolant. Its main drawback was cost: far more expensive to build than, say, Chevy's 265.

Even so, the Red Ram combined with surprisingly low weight to make the '53 Dodges not only terrific stormers but fine handlers and even frugal with fuel. A Red Ram scored 23.4 miles per gallon in the '53 Mobilgas Economy

1951 Dodge Wayfarer Sportabout convertible coupe

1953 Dodge Coronet Eight convertible coupe

1954 Dodge Royal 500 Official Pace Car convertible

1954 Dodge Royal Sport Coupe hardtop (spring model)

Run. Other V-8 Dodges broke 196 AAA stock-car records at Bonneville that year, and Danny Eames drove one to a record 102.62 mph on California's El Mirage dry lake.

Several interesting show cars also contributed to Dodge's now increasingly youthful image. Like others at Chrysler Corporation in this period, these Exner designs were built by Ghia in Italy. The first was Firearrow, a non-running '53 roadster made road-ready the following year. In late 1954 came an evolutionary Firearrow convertible and sport coupe, whose lines inspired the limited-production Dual-Ghia of 1956. The coupe proved quite aerodynamically stable, achieving 143.44 mph on the banked oval at the Chrysler Proving Grounds.

Only detail appearance changes occurred on Dodge's '54 production models, but the Red Ram became available across the board, and a luxurious new top-line Royal V-8 series bowed with club coupe, sedan, convertible, and Sport hardtop coupe. Meadowbrook now offered six and V-8 sedans and club coupes on the 119-inch chassis; Coronet added long-chassis four-door Sierra wagons and short two-door Suburbans, plus convertible and Sport hardtop as before.

Dodge paced the '54 Indy 500, and trumpeted its selection with 701 replica pace-car convertibles called Royal 500. Priced at $2632 each, they sported Kelsey-Hayes chrome wire wheels, "continental" outside spare tire, special ornamentation, and a tuned 150-bhp Red Ram. A dealer-installed four-barrel Offenhauser manifold was also available, which must have made this a screamer, though Chrysler never quoted actual horsepower.

The Royal 500 symbolized Dodge's rapid emergence as Chrysler's "performance" outfit. And indeed, the division was already rolling up competition victories. Lincoln is famous for its dominance in the Mexican Road Race of these years. Less widely known is the fact that Dodge overwhelmed the event's Medium Stock class in 1954, finishing 1-2-3-4-6-9.

After suffering in a poor sales year for all Chrysler products, Dodge came back with bigger, brighter, all-new '55s on a single 120-inch wheelbase. Styling, the work of Exner colleague Maury Baldwin, was flashy but not garish (though optional tri-tone paint jobs were conspicuous on some models), part of Chrysler's first-generation "Forward Look." Series comprised six and V-8 Coronets and V-8 Royals and Custom Royals. The last was the new line-topper, offering a basic four-door sedan and three Lancer sub-models: sedan, convertible, and hardtop coupe.

The old six, upped to 110 bhp for '54, now delivered 123 bhp, and a Red Ram bored out to 270.1 cid (3.63 × 3.25) delivered 175/183 bhp; an optional "Power Package" with four-barrel carb lifted that to 195. Dodge prospered with greatly increased '55 volume—nearly 277,000—but rivals also did well in that record industry year, and Dodge couldn't budge from eighth place.

An interesting '55 footnote was La Femme, a special limited-edition Custom Royal Lancer hardtop painted pink and white. As the name implied, it sported accoutrements for m'lady, including a folding umbrella and a

1955 Dodge Custom Royal Lancer convertible coupe

1956 Dodge Custom Royal Lancer La Femme hardtop coupe

1956 Dodge Royal Lancer D-500 hardtop coupe

1957 Dodge Coronet Lancer hardtop coupe

1958 Dodge Coronet Lancer hardtop coupe

1957 Dodge Sierra four-door station wagon

fitted handbag stored in the back of a front seat. La Femme returned for '56 (the women's movement was still many years away), but though briefly considered for volume sale, no more than a handful were produced.

All Chrysler products grew tailfins for '56, and Dodge wore them as well as any. Two-speed PowerFlite, the firm's first fully automatic transmission, had arrived with dashboard lever control in '54. Now it had pushbuttons, in a handy pod left of the wheel.

Besides revised frontal styling and new interiors, Dodge '56 also advertised a stroked "Super Red Ram" V-8 with 315 cid (3.63 × 3.80) and 218 bhp, versus 189 for the returning 270. The evergreen six now delivered 131 horses. Available across the board was the first of the now-famous "D-500" options. For 1956 this was just a four-barrel carb that provided 230 bhp. However, Chrysler's own pictorial history also lists a four-barrel 315 with higher compression (9.25:1 vs. 8.0 elsewhere), good for 260 bhp.

Other '56 developments involved a new Lancer four-door hardtop sedan in each series, and a "spring special" Golden Lancer, a D-500 Custom Royal hardtop coupe with Sapphire White/Gallant Gold exterior and harmonizing white/black/gray interior.

Nineteen fifty-six was a down year for all Detroit, and Dodge built 240,000 cars to again run eighth. But helped by torsion-bar suspension, all-new styling, and more power for '57, Dodge would climb to seventh as volume swelled to nearly 288,000.

Carrying Exner's all-new "second generation" Forward Look, the '57 Dodges were longer, lower, wider, and more aggressive-looking, with a massive bumper/grille, lots of glass and high-flying fins. (Ads called this "Swept-Wing" styling.) Wheelbase stretched to 122 inches, where it would remain through 1960. The Hemi was again enlarged: bored out this time to 325 cid (3.69 × 3.80). The result, depending on compression and carbs, was 245-310

1959 Dodge Custom Royal four-door sedan

1959 Dodge Custom Royal Lancer convertible coupe

arrived as one of the "spring specials" so long favored by Chrysler marketers. Some of its trim items were also available on lesser models, including lancer-head grille medallion, blackout headlamp trim, and rather contrived bodyside and fin moldings. Sensibly left alone were 1957's new Torsion-Aire Ride and optional three-speed TorqueFlite automatic transmission, which had earned near-universal praise—and buyer approval. Both would persist at Dodge and throughout the corporate camp for many years.

Now in its final season, Dodge's 325 Hemi packed 252/265 bhp for '58. The new wedgehead 361 (4.12 × 3.38) delivered 305, 320, or the aforementioned 333 bhp. A smaller 350 version offered 295 standard bhp in Custom Royals and V-8 wagons. Though 1958 was disastrous for every Detroit make, Dodge fared worse than most. Model-year production plunged to 138,000 as the division barely finished ahead of Cadillac.

Sharing in a modest 1959 recovery, Dodge built about 156,000 cars and returned from ninth to eighth place in the volume stakes. Contributing to this less-than-sterling performance was a rather heavy-handed facelift with droopy hooded headlamps, plus misshapen fins above suggestive thrusting taillamps. Revised interiors could be newly furnished with swivel front seats, semi-buckets that pivoted outward on opening a door. The venerable flathead six was in its final year. V-8s, now exclusively wedgeheads, comprised a new 326 (3.95 × 3.31) with 255 bhp for Coronets; a 305-bhp 361 for other models, and a big new 383 (4.25 × 3.38) with 320/345 bhp. The last-named was that year's D-500—and not cheap. The four-barrel 305-bhp unit cost $304 extra; the Super version with twin four-barrels ran $446. Both were thirsty, but it was the age of 30-cents-a-gallon gas and the market still craved performance (if not quite as much as before the '58 recession).

Of course, the market has always craved performance—always will—and Dodge has continued to satisfy that hunger. Today we have a new generation of hot Dodges led by the electrifying Viper RT/10 and the slick Intrepid ES sedan, all bearing a revived "ram's head" logo straight from the Fifties. That, we think, not only indicates where Dodge is headed, but suggests that for car enthusiasts, the "good old days" aren't necessarily in the past.

bhp. The '57 D-500 option was a 354 from the junior Chryslers, tuned for 340 bhp. The old six got another six horses for its ultimate total of 138.

The D-500 package was Dodge's alternative to its sister divisions' limited-edition supercars, available for any model right down to the plain-Jane Coronet two-door. Shocks, springs, and the new-for-'57 front torsion bars were all suitably firmed up for what *Motor Trend* magazine called "close liaison with the road"—handling that put D-500s at the head of the class. V-8s delivered brisk to blistering go. Even the relatively mild 245-bhp mill typically delivered 0-60 in about 9.5 seconds. The D-500 continued into 1958-59, but with 361- and 383-cid wedgehead V-8s instead of the expensive Hemi. With optional Bendix fuel injection offered only for '58, the 361 delivered an impressive 333 bhp.

A mild facelift with four headlamps and revised trim marked the '58 Dodges. The lineup was a rerun until February, when a spiffy Regal Lancer hardtop coupe

	DODGE AT A GLANCE									
Model Year	**1950**	**1951**	**1952**	**1953**	**1954**	**1955**	**1956**	**1957**	**1958**	**1959**
Price Range, $	1629-2883	1813-2934	1904-3082	1983-2528	1983-3031	2013-2761	2194-2913	2370-3670	2449-3354	2516-3439
Weight Range, Lbs.	3095-4045	3175-3935	3050-3935	3085-3480	3120-3660	3235-3730	3250-3715	3400-4030	3360-4035	3375-4020
Wheelbases, Ins.	115-137.5	115-137.5	115-137.5	114-119	114-119	120	120	122	122	122
6 Cyl. Engines, BHP	103	103	103	103	110	123	131	138	138	135
8 Cyl. Engines, BHP				140	140, 150	175, 193	189-260	245-340	252-333	255-345

A comedy of errors, or a good idea at the wrong time? The Edsel was both—proof that what seems sound today may not be so tomorrow. As one historian later wrote of Edsel: "Its aim was right, but the target moved."

That aim was sighted in the heady climate of 1954, when Ford Motor Company had recovered strongly from its near-collapse of the late Forties. Led by board chairman Ernest R. Breech, optimistic Dearborn managers, determined to match General Motors model for model, laid expansionist plans for a GM-like five-make hierarchy involving a separate new Continental Division (see "Continental") and a second medium-price make to bolster Mercury. The latter made appealing sense at a time when medium-price car sales were booming. In record-setting 1955, for example, Pontiac, Buick, and Dodge built nearly two million cars combined.

But with the industry's usual three-year lead times, Edsel didn't arrive until late 1957, by which point the entire market was depressed and medium-price sales had shriveled from 25 percent to about 18. Edsel Division hoped to sell 100,000 of its debut '58s, but built only a little over 63,000. That was actually pretty good, all things considered. Trouble was, it wouldn't get better. Thus, after fewer than 45,000 for '59 and a token 3000 cars for 1960, Edsel was summarily canceled.

The name, of course, honored the only son of company founder Henry Ford and the father of then-president Henry Ford II. But it was hardly the first choice. Ford solicited monikers from all over—including poetess Marianne Moore, who came up with stunners like "Mongoose Civique," "Turcotinga," and "Utopian Turtletop." Ranger, Pacer, Corsair, and Citation ended up the top finishers among 6000 names considered by the ad agency, and were ultimately adopted as series designations. But Breech didn't like these or any of the other suggestions. "Edsel" had popped up as an early prospect, probably because the project was known as the "E-car" within the Special Products Division. But the Ford family was against it, and even publicly denied it would ever be used. When a decision lagged, however, Breech stepped in. "I'll take care of Henry," he declared. He did, and Edsel it was.

Though originally conceived as a more expensive and powerful "super Mercury," Edsel was positioned between Mercury and Ford. It was also not the radical all-new design rumored by the press for some two years before introduction.

The '58 line comprised Ranger and Pacer on the 118-inch wheelbase (116 for wagons) of the 1957-58 Ford; Corsair and Citation rode Mercury's 124-inch chassis. Bodyshells were similarly shared. Ranger offered two- and four-door sedans and hardtops, two-door Roundup wagons, and four-door Villager wagons with seating for six or nine. Pacer deleted the two-door wagon and sedan but added a convertible and two woody-look Bermuda wagons. Corsair was limited to pillarless coupe and sedan; Citation offered these plus a soft-top. Prices were about $500 below comparable Mercurys, in the $2500-$3800 range.

Styling was the '58 Edsel's most unique aspect—and the most controversial, especially the "horse-collar" vertical grille (which was called worse by its detractors) and slim, near-horizontal "gullwing" taillights (which one cynic likened to "ingrown toenails"). At least those lights obviated fins, and the entire package was tastefully restrained next to the glittery '58 Buick and Olds. Typical of the day, gadgets abounded: optional "Teletouch Drive" automatic transmission controlled by pushbuttons in the steering wheel hub; "cyclops eye" drum-type speedometer; power assists for everything except doors and rearview mirror.

Power centered on two V-8s from Dearborn's new 1958 "FE-series" big-block family. Ranger/Pacer carried a 361 cubic-inch unit (bore and stroke: 4.05×3.50 inches) with 303 horsepower; Corsair/Citation relied on a massive 410 (4.20×3.70) with 345 bhp. With that, Edsels were quite rapid, but roadability and braking left much to be desired, also typical of the times.

Disappointing first-year sales dictated a reduced platoon of '59 Edsels on a single 120-inch wheelbase—basically reskinned Fords. Offerings comprised Villager wagons seating six or nine, Corsair convertible, Ranger two-door sedan, and Corsair/Ranger four-door sedans, hardtop coupes and hardtop sedans.

Engines proliferated, though. Rangers and Villagers came with a 292 V-8 (3.75×3.30) offering 200 bhp, but a 145-bhp 223-cid inline six (3.62×3.60) was a new no-charge option, nodding to the market's newfound concern for fuel economy with the '58 recession. Corsairs had a

1958 Edsel Citation convertible coupe

1958 Edsel Citation convertible coupe

1959 Edsel Corsair convertible coupe

1959 Edsel Corsair hardtop sedan

1959 Edsel Ranger two-door sedan

standard 225-bhp 332 V-8 (4.00 × 3.30), again from Ford Division. The 361 returned unchanged as a linewide option ($58)—but in the lighter '59s it delivered 0-60-mph acceleration of 10 seconds or less. Styling was toned-down from '58, with grille-mounted headlights, taller windshields, and more conventional taillights moved down into the back panel. Prices were trimmed along

EDSEL AT A GLANCE				
Model Year	1950	1951	1958	1959
Price Range, $			2519-3801	2629-3072
Weight Range, Lbs.			3724-4311	3547-3842
Wheelbases, Ins.			116-124	120
6 Cyl. Engines, BHP				145
8 Cyl. Engines, BHP			303-345	200-303

with models and weight. The costliest '59, the ragtop Corsair, started at about $3100.

Dearborn halted Edsel production in November of 1959, but not before a halfhearted run of downpriced, "de-contented" 1960 cars that were even more Ford-like than the '59s. They were also fewer in number: just two Villagers and five Rangers. It's a wonder any of them got built—and some nearly didn't. The line-topping Ranger convertible saw but 76 copies, the three-seat Villager a mere 59.

Thus ended Detroit's biggest and most public flop since the Tucker. Nowadays, "Edsel" shows up in dictionaries as a synonym for "loser"—unfortunate considering the great legacy of Edsel Ford. But though Ford reportedly spent $250 million on the project, it wasn't a total loss. Plant expansion for Edsel production left Ford with a surplus that came in very handy when its new 1960 Falcon immediately ran away with the compact market.

Had it been a truly different car introduced three to five years either side of 1958, the Edsel might be with us yet. Instead, it stands as a monument to the cynicism of a time when Detroit thought buyers didn't know—or care about—the difference between style and substance.

Ford Motor Company might not have survived the Fifties had the all-new '49 Ford sold any less well than it did. At the time of its June 1948 introduction, young Henry Ford II was still feeling his way as company president—and still scrambling to bring order to the organizational and fiscal chaos he inherited from his grandfather even as Dearborn continued to lose money by the bucketful.

But the '49 was the most changed Ford since the Model A, and as much a sensation. Strong sales—over 1.1 million for that extended model year—averted disaster. By 1952, Ford had regained its traditional number-two spot in industry production, helped in no small measure by a faltering Chrysler Corporation.

The '49 Ford was a rush job, due to a last-minute change in management thinking, but had more than enough of the "right stuff." Against the 1946-48 models it boasted a modern ladder-type frame with Dearborn's first fully independent front suspension, plus a modern rear end with open Hotchkiss drive (replacing torque-tube) and parallel leaf springs. Wheelbase was unchanged at 115 inches, but the '49 was three inches lower, fractionally shorter, and usefully lighter, yet even roomier inside. Despite the altered dimensions, neat new slab-sided styling—the work of moonlighting Studebaker talents Bob Bourke and Holden "Bob" Koto—made for a pleasingly sleeker look. Engines were unchanged too, but didn't need to be. These were, of course, Ford's famous flathead V-8, still at 100 horsepower from 239.4 cubic inches (bore and stroke: 3.19 × 3.75 inches), and the L-head six that dated from just before the war, again making 95 bhp from 226 cid (3.30 × 4.40).

It all added up to a sprightly performer that could run circles around rival Chevys and Plymouths. A Ford still couldn't quite reach 100 mph, but hopping up the flathead V-8 remained simple, cheap, and easy.

Efforts for 1950 aimed at quashing the handling, noise, and workmanship bugs that stemmed from the '49's rushed development. "50 Ways New, 50 Ways Better," blared the ads. And the 1950s *were* better: discernibly tighter and quieter in corners and rough-road driving alike. Offerings, as for '49, split between base DeLuxe and uplevel Custom series. DeLuxe listed "Tudor" and "Fordor" sedans and a long-deck club coupe sans back seat for business use. Custom offered a conventional coupe and a convertible, plus a two-door structural-wood wagon newly advertised as "Country Squire." A special new 1950 confection was the V-8 Crestliner, a limited-edition Tudor designed to counter Chevy's Bel Air hardtop. A contrasting bodyside color sweep and padded vinyl top made it snazzy, but only 17,601 were sold for 1950, followed by 8703 of the '51s.

Ford's 1950 styling was predictably much like '49's, though a crest instead of Ford lettering above the "bullet" grille provided instant identification. Prices held steady, running from $1333 for the DeLuxe business coupe to $2028 for the Squire. Though still without a true hardtop and fully automatic transmission to counter archrival Chevrolet, Ford recorded its highest model-year car pro-

1950 Ford DeLuxe Tudor sedan

1950 Ford Custom Crestliner Tudor sedan

duction since 1930: over 1.2 million. But Chevrolet managed close to 1.5 million, and would remain "USA-1."

An attractive facelift gave the '51 Fords a new grille with small twin bullets on a thick horizontal bar. The Country Squire now wore its name in script, but this would be the last year for true Ford "woodys." The Crestliner was also saying goodbye. That's because Ford now had the Custom V-8 Victoria, a true hardtop. Though a year behind Chevy's Bel Air, it was even more popular, some 110,000 finding buyers. Arriving with it was three-speed Ford-O-Matic Drive, a full automatic to match Chevy's Powerglide. Ford's model-year volume declined some 200,000 cars, but Chevy's fell a similar amount, reflecting new government-ordered restrictions on civilian production prompted by the Korean War.

Model-year '52 introduced a clean new square-rigged Ford with one-piece windshield, simple grille, neat round taillamps, and an "air scoop" motif on the lower rear flanks. Only detail changes would occur to this basic design through 1954. Wheelbase remained 115 inches for a revised model slate that began with cheap Mainline Tudor/Fordor sedans, business coupe, and two-door

1951 Ford Custom Country Squire two-door station wagon

1951 Ford Custom Victoria hardtop coupe

1952 Ford Crestline Sunliner convertible coupe

1953 Ford Crestline Victoria hardtop coupe

1954 Ford Crestline Skyliner hardtop coupe

Ranch Wagon, followed by Customline sedans, club coupe, and four-door Country Sedan wagon. Leading the line was a V-8 Crestline group of Victoria hardtop, newly named Sunliner convertible, and the posh Country Squire four-door wagon. These wagons, by the way, were Ford's first all-steel models, with the Squire switching from real wood to wood-look decals. Doing more with less, Ford introduced a new 101-bhp overhead-valve six of 215.3 cid (3.56 × 3.60) as standard for Mainline/Customline; the venerable flathead V-8 was coaxed up to 110 bhp.

Ford Motor Company observed its Golden Anniversary in 1953, and proclaimed it on Fords with special steering-wheel hub medallions. But other than that and some minor appearance alterations, the '53s were basically '52s with higher prices: now in the $1400-$2200 range. With the Korean conflict ended, Ford Division built 1.2 million cars for the model year, then would beat that with nearly 1.5 million for banner '55. Ford was closing in on Chevy, but straining its dealers by overloading them with cars in a forced production "blitz."

Ford's venerable flathead V-8 was honorably retired for 1954 in favor of a new overhead-valve "Y-block" V-8. With 130 bhp, it was easily the hottest engine in the low-price field. Together with ball-joint front suspension, also new that year, it greatly narrowed the engineering gap between expensive and inexpensive cars. Its initial 239 cid was the same as flathead displacement, but the ohv had entirely different "oversquare" bore/stroke dimensions (3.50 × 3.10). Compression was 7.2:1 in standard trim, but could be taken as high as 12:1.

The rest of the '54 story was basically a '53 reprise except for a larger, 223-cid ohv six (3.62 × 3.60) with 115 bhp, plus a novel new hardtop, the Skyliner. This was basically the Crestline Victoria with a transparent, green-tint Plexiglas roof insert over the front seat. A forerunner of today's moonroof, it cast a bilious interior pall, and heat buildup was a problem. This and a price identical with the convertible's—$2164—limited '54 Skyliner sales to only 13,344 units.

Retaining the 1952-54 shell, the '55 Ford was completely reskinned, emerging colorful if chromey, with a rakish look of motion and a modestly wrapped windshield. Styling was handled by Franklin Q. Hershey, who also gets credit for this year's new Thunderbird, which is detailed further on in this volume. In the passenger line, club coupes were abandoned, station wagons became a separate series, and Crestline was renamed Fairlane (after the Ford family estate). With the "horsepower race" in full swing, Ford ousted the 239 V-8 for a 272-cid enlargement (3.62 × 3.30) with 162/182 bhp.

Replacing Skyliner for '55 was the $2272 Fairlane Crown Victoria, a hardtop-style two-door with a vee'd chrome band wrapped over the roof from rakishly angled B-posts. The band looked like a roll bar, but added little, if any, strength. The Plexiglas insert rode ahead of it. A steel-roof model was also offered at a $70 saving, and sold much better than the "bubbletopper": 33,000-plus to just 1999. The totals were 9209 and just 603 for '56, after which the Crown Vic was dropped.

A mild facelift and more powerful engines were Ford's main news for '56, but there were two new models: a Customline Victoria and a Fairlane Town Victoria hardtop sedan. Ford began selling "Lifeguard Design" safety features, equipping all models with dished steering wheel, breakaway rearview mirror, and crashproof door locks; padded dash and sunvisors cost $16 extra, factory-installed seatbelts $9.

The 272 V-8 delivered 173 bhp as a '56 Mainline/Customline option. Optional across the board was a new "Thunderbird" 312 V-8 (3.80 × 3.44) with 215/225 bhp. Also new was a mid-range 200-bhp 292 (3.75 × 3.30).

The '57 Fords were all-new, offering a vast array of V-8s from a 190-bhp 272 up to a 245-bhp 312. The 223-cid six was standard for all but one model. Offerings now spanned two wheelbases and five series: 116 inches for wagons and Custom/Custom 300 sedans (replacing Mainline/Customline), 118 inches for Fairlane and a new line-topping Fairlane 500 series. All were available with six or V-8 power. Both Fairlane series listed two- and four-door Victorias, plus thin-pillar equivalents that looked like hardtops with windows up. The glamorous drop-top Sunliner was now a Fairlane 500. Wagons comprised plain and fancier Del Rio two-door Ranch Wagons, a pair of four-door Country Sedans, and the woody-look four-door Squire, which was Ford's priciest '57 at $2684.

Ford's '57 styling was particularly simple for the period: a blunt face with a clean, full-width rectangular grille; rakish side moldings; tiny tailfins. More importantly, it was new at a year when Chevy facelifted for the second year in a row. Alas, the cars had some structural weaknesses (roof panels were the main one) and were prone to rust—one reason you don't see many today. But though Plymouth arguably won the styling stakes with its finned Forward Look, 1957 was a great Ford year. In fact, Ford scored a substantial victory in model-year production with close to 1.7 million cars to Chevy's 1.5 million.

The Skyliner name returned at mid-1957, though on a very different Ford: the world's first mass-produced retractable hardtop, an addition to the Fairlane 500 line. It stemmed from earlier developmental engineering at Continental Division, which had considered, but didn't produce, the 1956 Mark II as a "retrac." Ford sold 20,766 Skyliners for '57, but demand quickly tapered to 14,713 for '58, then to 12,915. The model was then duly axed.

For 1958, Ford countered all-new passenger Chevys and modestly restyled Plymouths with a glittery facelift featuring quad headlamps and taillamps, a '58 Thunderbird-style bumper/grille, and more anodized aluminum trim. V-8 choices expanded via two new "FE-series" big-blocks: a 332 (4.00 × 3.30) offering 240/265 bhp, and a 300-bhp 352 (4.00 × 3.50). A deep national recession cut Ford volume to just under 988,000 units.

Chevrolet returned with an all-new line of radical "bat-fin" models for '59. Ford replied with more conservative styling that helped it close the model-year gap to less than 12,000 units. A major reskin of the basic '57 platform featured squared-up body lines with simple side moldings, a heavily sculptured back panel, and a low, rectangular

1955 Ford Fairlane Club Sedan two-door

1955 Ford Thunderbird convertible coupe

1956 Ford Fairlane Crown Victoria hardtop coupe

1956 Ford Customline Victoria hardtop coupe

1957 Ford Thunderbird convertible coupe

1957 Ford Fairlane 500 Victoria hardtop sedan

1958 Ford Fairlane 500 Victoria hardtop coupe

1959 Ford Thunderbird hardtop coupe

1959 Ford Galaxie Sunliner convertible coupe

grille filled with floating star-like ornaments. All previous models carried over, though now on the 118-inch wheelbase. Come mid-season, though, a new Galaxie series of two- and four-door pillared and pillarless sedans generated high buyer interest and strong sales with their stylish wide-quarter rooflines. At the same time, the Sunliner convertible and Skyliner retrac gained Galaxie rear-fender script (but retained Fairlane 500 I.D. at the rear). V-8s were down to a 200-bhp 292, 225-bhp 332, and 300-bhp 352. Also carried over from '58 was Cruise-O-Matic, Ford's smooth new three-speed automatic that proved a selling point against two-speed Chevy Powerglide, if not Plymouth's responsive three-speed TorqueFlite.

For Ford Motor Company as a whole, 1959 justified the strenuous efforts of Henry Ford II and board chairman Ernest Breech. Assuming control of a third-rate company in 1945, they'd turned it into something approaching General Motors in less than 15 years.

No car better symbolized Dearborn's resurgence than the Thunderbird, the "personal-luxury" Ford first offered in two-seat form for 1955. Legend says it was born in October 1951, when Ford Division general manager Lewis Crusoe visited the Paris Auto Show with styling consultant George Walker. America had fallen in love with European sports cars in the early postwar years, and both men were taken by the two-seaters they saw at Paris—especially the curvy Jaguar XK-120 and GM's experimental LeSabre. "Why don't we have something like that?" Crusoe asked. "Oh, but we do," replied Walker—who then hurried to phone home to get his crew cracking.

But this story is apocryphal. Frank Hershey, who led the original styling team, says Ford had been conjuring two-seaters before 1951, though there was never a rush to build one because sports cars then accounted for only a minuscule 0.27 percent of the total U.S. market. But in January 1953, GM threw down a gauntlet Ford couldn't ignore: the Chevrolet Corvette. Barely a month later, Ford was hard at work on the car ultimately named for the god worshipped by America's Southwest Indians as the bringer of rain and prosperity.

Unveiled as a wood mockup at the Detroit show in early 1954, the Thunderbird was sporty, but not a pure sports car. It rode the same wheelbase as the first-generation Corvette—102 inches—but was far more luxurious and practical. In place of creaking fiberglass and clumsy side curtains was a sturdy steel body with convenient roll-up windows. Instead of an ill-fitting soft top was a snug power top, a detachable hard top, or both. And there was no plodding six-cylinder engine but a burly 292 Mercury V-8 packing 193 bhp with stickshift or 198 bhp with Ford-O-Matic.

Bill Burnett supervised engineering, which relied heavily on standard passenger-Ford components. Styling, executed under Hershey's direction by young Bill Boyer, couldn't have been better: simple and smooth yet clearly Ford, with rakish long-hood/short-deck proportions recalling the classic early-Forties Lincoln Continental.

With its European style and American comfort, convenience, and go, Thunderbird proved well-nigh irresistible at just under $3000 without options. To no one's surprise, it soundly whipped the rival Corvette in 1955-model production by nearly 24 to 1— a total 16,155.

You don't mess with success in Detroit, and Ford didn't with the '56 T-Bird. Changes were limited to a larger 312 V-8 option with 215/225 bhp (non-overdrive stickshift cars retained the 292, now with 202 bhp), plus an exterior-mount spare (answering cries for more trunk space), softer suspension (for a smoother ride), and no-cost portholes for the hardtop, a Thirties idea suggested by Boyer. Porthole hardtops heavily outsold the non-porthole kind in 1956, and virtually all '57 Thunderbirds had them. Production eased to 15,631 but was still five times Corvette's. Trouble was, new division chief Bob McNamara, one of the "Whiz Kids" who'd helped save Dearborn from extinction, wanted much higher volume. Then too, market surveys showed much greater interest in a four-seater, which debuted for '58.

But the last two-seat Bird was arguably the best: handsomely facelifted with a prominent bumper/grille and a longer deck (again enclosing the spare) wearing modest blade-like tailfins. Horsepower was higher than ever. Stickshift cars again carried a 292 V-8, albeit uprated to 212 bhp, and three 312 options offered 245, 270, or 285 bhp, the last being the top twin-four-barrel version with 10.0:1 compression. Ford also built 208 supercharged "F-Birds" with 300/340 bhp.

And "early Birds" did race, though with limited success. A '55 sponsored by *Mechanix Illustrated* magazine's Tom McCahill swept the production sports-car class at that year's Daytona Speed Weeks, Joe Ferguson's two-way average of 124.633 mph besting every Austin-Healey, Porsche, and all but one Jaguar XK-120. Chuck Daigh did even better in '56 with a car prepped by Pete DePaolo, running 88.779 mph in the standing mile; still, Zora Arkus-Duntov's modified 'Vette was faster (89.735 mph). In '57, Daigh scored 93.312 mph, and a privately entered Bird ran the flying mile at 146.282 mph one way, 138.775 mph both ways.

With a base price still under $3500 for '57, the T-Bird remained an attractive buy. Production ran through the end of the calendar year, so production was the highest of the three two-seat models: 21,380 units.

Design and manufacturing problems delayed the expected four-seat Thunderbird until January 1958—after which Ford couldn't build 'em fast enough. Dramatically styled, with a low, rakish stance, it strode a longer but still fairly compact 113-inch wheelbase, which provided decent interior space on a quartet of individual "buckety" seats. Suspension switched from rear-leaf to all-coil. Construction went from body-on-frame to unitized, which allowed the bigger Bird to be built alongside 1958's huge new "unibody" Lincolns and Continentals at a specially dedicated plant in Wixom, Michigan.

One engine was offered for the '58 T-Bird: the new 300-bhp big-block 352 V-8 from that year's passenger Fords. But the familiar convertible now had a companion, a fixed-roof hardtop whose square-cut roofline would be picked up by Ford's '59 Galaxies—and other automakers. A Skyliner-style retractable was canceled in the design stage, but a similar top-stowing mechanism was used on the convertible, which didn't go on sale until April 1958. Also destined to be widely imitated was the new Bird's control console atop the transmission tunnel.

Though a restyled two-seater was briefly considered for the '58 program, the four-seat Bird needed no sales help. Despite an abbreviated model year, nearly 38,000 found buyers, about twice as many as any of the two-seaters.

Predictably, the "Squarebird," as collectors have since termed it, changed only in detail for '59: a horizontal-bar instead of honeycomb pattern for grille, taillight surrounds, and the non-functioning hood air scoop; "bullet" moldings for the sculptured lower-body "bombs"; reworked name script; and bird logos on the hardtop's rear roof pillars (instead of round emblems). Lincoln's 350-bhp 430 V-8 (4.30 × 3.70), listed but likely never installed for '58, became a full option. The '59 bested the '58 in production with 67,500 units.

In retrospect, Ford Division's high Fifties success stemmed from astute and timely product decisions, bolstered by consistently good styling (with the '58 passenger line an arguable exception) and more than competitive performance. Ford also benefited from its interesting Crestliners, Skyliners, Crown Victorias, and Thunderbirds. Though always peripheral to sales and profits, these cars had great value as showroom draws for prospective Ford buyers, who usually ended up being Ford owners.

FORD AT A GLANCE										
Model Year	1950	1951	1952	1953	1954	1955	1956	1957	1958	1959
Price Range, $	1332-2262	1424-2253	1526-2384	1537-2403	1548-2415	1606-2944	1748-3151	1879-3408	1967-3929	2132-3979
Weight Range, Lbs.	2965-3510	2960-3550	2984-3640	2987-3609	3021-3684	2980-3605	3032-3638	3141-3689	3171-4069	3283-4064
Wheelbases, Ins.	114	114	115	115	115.5 115.5	102, 115.5	102, 118	102-118	113-118	113, 118
6 Cyl. Engines, BHP	95	95	101	101	115	120	137	144	145	145
8 Cyl. Engines, BHP	100	100	110	110	130	162-198	173-225	190-300	205-300	200-350

Frazer breathed its last in 1951 after a short, somewhat unhappy life. The name honored Joseph Washington Frazer, a high-born aristocrat (descended from the Virginia Washingtons) who loved motorcars and became a super-salesman through stints at Packard, Pierce-Arrow, and General Motors. Frazer also worked with Walter P. Chrysler in the Twenties and resuscitated moribund Willys-Overland in the late Thirties.

A few years later, Frazer was looking to build a new postwar car, an idea that also occurred to Henry J. Kaiser, the West Coast metals and construction tycoon who'd also turned out Liberty ships double-quick in wartime. Frazer and Kaiser met, hit it off, and formed Kaiser-Frazer Corporation in July 1945, with Frazer as president and Kaiser as board chairman.

They considered several products, then settled on a conventional front-engine four-door sedan with modern flush-fender styling by renowned custom-body designer Howard A. "Dutch" Darrin. Two versions were planned: a medium-priced Kaiser and a luxury Frazer. Henry J, thinking big as usual, geared up for Kaisers by buying Ford's huge, wartime bomber factory in Willow Run, Michigan. Frazers were to be built by Graham-Paige in Detroit, lately acquired by Joe and his associates, but G-P was foundering and sold out to K-F, so all but very early Frazers were built alongside Kaisers.

Both makes began production in June 1946 (for model-year '47). Each offered basic and upmarket models. The Kaisers were called Special and Custom; Frazers were nameless "Standards" and Manhattans. There was only one engine: a long-stroke 226.2 cubic-inch flathead six (bore and stroke: 3.31 × 4.38 inches), the Continental "Red Seal" design built by K-F. Frazer advertised it as the "Supersonic Six," but with only 100/110 horsepower to push over 3300 pounds, no K-F car acted jet-propelled. At least the Darrin design offered exceptional interior room.

Initially, K-F built one two Kaisers to each Frazer, reflecting the latter's higher $2295 starting price—close to Cadillac territory. The Manhattan was some $400 more, but was elegantly upholstered in nylon and fine Bedford cord cloth keyed to exterior colors.

Despite that—and no eight-cylinder engine in sight—K-F enjoyed instant sales success, earning the press sobriquet of "postwar wonder company." Still, some observers doubted its dynamic managerial duo. Henry Kaiser, they said, didn't know an automobile from a motorboat, while Frazer had only sold cars, not built them.

Even so, K-F succeeded despite postwar materials shortages, forming a crack team of expediters who foraged the country for everything from sheet steel to copper wire. They usually got what they wanted—though at a price, the main reason the cars cost so much. Still, K-F racked up the highest output of any independent in 1947-48, sufficient for ninth place in the production race.

The '48 models changed only in detail yet cost even more: $2483-$2746. The '49 Frazers took on an eggcrate grille, prominent rectangular parking lamps, and large two-lens vertical taillamps. There was also a new four-door Manhattan convertible, but it was a makeshift job at

1950 Frazer Manhattan four-door sedan

1951 Frazer Manhattan hardtop sedan

best. Directed to do or die, engineers John Widman and Ralph Isbrandt sheared the top off a sedan, put little glass panes where the door pillars were, and purchased beefed-up X-member frames at an inordinate price. But at over $3000, the four-door floptop Frazer simply couldn't sell in viable numbers. Nor could any '49 Frazer. As a result, some 5000 '49 leftovers were reserialed for a brief 1950 run that ended in the spring of that year.

Frazer's 1951 output was abbreviated too, but the cars looked startlingly different, thanks to an effective front and rear redo by K-F Styling's Herb Weissinger. The intent was to use up remaining 1949-50 bodyshells. Thus, leftover Kaiser Vagabond utility sedans (with double hatchback and folding rear seat) became standard-trim '51 Frazer Vagabonds, while Kaiser Virginian four-door "hardtops" were made into '51 Frazer Manhattan models. Pillared sedans were assigned to the standard Frazer line, but trimmed like 1950 Manhattans. Helped by the belated arrival of Hydra-Matic as a $159 option, dealers ordered 55,000 of the '51 Frazers, but received only 10,214. The Frazer was dead.

FRAZER AT A GLANCE		
Model Year	**1950**	**1951**
Price Range, $	2395-3295	2359-3075
Weight Range, Lbs.	3386-3726	3456-3941
Wheelbases, Ins.	123.5	123.5
6 Cyl. Engines, BHP	112	115

Kaiser-Frazer went from the "postwar wonder" of 1947-48 to looking like a postwar blunder in 1949, falling from ninth to 14th in Detroit production. Determined to press on regardless, chairman Henry J. Kaiser borrowed $44 million from the Reconstruction Finance Corporation to maintain inventories, then tooled up for new models. One result was the abrupt departure of co-founder Joseph W. Frazer. Kaiser promised the RFC that part of its money would go toward a new small car that any American could afford. With no little modesty, he named it the Henry J.

Designer Howard A. "Dutch" Darrin had proposed a short-wheelbase compact derived from his beautiful 1951 Kaiser, which was already locked up during Henry J planning. But the head man, wanting something all-new, went with a proposal from American Metal Products, a Detroit supplier of frames and springs for car seats. Darrin reluctantly tried to improve this ungainly little two-door fastback sedan, applying his trademark "dip" to beltline, windshield, and rear window, plus little tailfins. The result was still pretty weird, but The New York Fashion Academy named Henry J its 1951 "Fashion Car of the Year."

Power was provided by Willys L-head engines: a 134 cubic-inch four (bore and stroke: 3.13 × 4.38 inches) and a 161-cid six (3.13 × 3.50). Incredible economy was promised by the 68-horsepower four, but the 80-bhp six turned out to be a hot rod, giving 0-60 times of around 14 seconds thanks mainly to the cars low weight (around 2300 pounds). Though built on a compact 100-inch wheelbase, the Henry J could handle four passengers and a considerable amount of luggage.

K-F began its '51 model year in March 1950. For a while, the Henry J was in demand: nearly 82,000 of the '51s were sold. But that evidently satisfied the market, for sales went down sharply through 1952. One reason was price. At $1363, even the four-cylinder model was only about $200 cheaper than a full-size six-cylinder Chevrolet—and far more basic. The six-cylinder version offered "DeLuxe" appointments starting at $1499, but was a little less stark.

A mild facelift gave the 1952-54 models a smart new full-width grille, taillights moved from body to the fins, and nicer interiors. An interim measure designed to use up leftover stock was the 1952 Vagabond—a '51 fitted with "continental" outside spare tire, identifying script, and a hood ornament of black plastic and chrome. After this, Henry Js were called Corsair or Corsair DeLuxe, and prices settled at $1400 for the four-cylinder version or $1560 with six.

But nothing seemed to work, so the Henry J departed in 1954. An estimated 1100 were sold that year, all reserialed '53 leftovers. Some 30,000 were built altogether.

Many observers felt the original approach was wrong. The '51s were austere, lacking gloveboxes, trunklids, and other features normally held essential—just too plain for most buyers. "I would have brought it out dressed up," commented Joe Frazer. And indeed, that's what Sears did with its short-lived Allstate version of this car (see "Allstate"). Then too, the market was not quite ready for com-

1951 Henry J two-door sedan

1953 Henry J Corsair two-door sedan

pacts (though it soon would be), and K-F was struggling mightily for survival by '54. Left stillborn were plans for a Henry J hardtop, wagon, four-door sedan, and even a convertible.

In all, this was a classic case of too little, too soon. Like Hudson's equally ill-starred Jet, the Henry J was the wrong car at the wrong time.

HENRY J AT A GLANCE				
Model Year	1951	1952	1953	1954
Price Range, $	1363-1499	1407-1664	1399-1561	1404-1566
Weight Range, Lbs.	2293-2341	2365-2405	2395-2445	2405-2455
Wheelbases, Ins.	100	100	100	100
4 Cyl. Engines, BHP	68	68	68	68
6 Cyl. Engines, BHP	80	80	80	80

Hudson expired in 1957, one year short of its 50th birthday. The reason was its radical "Step-Down" design, the great sales blessing of the late Forties that became an increasingly fatal curse in the Fifties.

Introduced for 1948 and named for its then-innovative recessed or dropped floorpan, the Step-Down completely surrounded passengers with strong frame girders in one of the safest automobiles of the day—maybe one of the safest ever. It also offered rattle-free unitized construction, a Hudson hallmark since 1932; a radically low center of gravity that made for great handling; and long wheelbases that made for a smooth ride and a king-size interior. With all this, Hudson enjoyed healthy profits and production: 117,200 of the '48 models, 144,685 of the near-identical '49s.

Trouble was, the Step-Down couldn't be greatly changed without great expense, and Hudson sales weren't sufficient to cover that once the postwar seller's market ended in 1950. A costly, ill-advised 1953-54 compact only further depleted dwindling cash reserves. As a result, Hudson couldn't afford to update the old late-Forties "torpedo" styling until 1954—when it was way too late—and would never get around to station wagons or V-8 engines, two very popular Fifties commodities. In fact, the Step-Down offered only six-cylinder power after 1952, and though the "fabulous" Hornet engine dominated stock-car racing for a time, sixes were tough to sell in the mostly eight-cylinder medium-price field where Hudson competed.

Roy D. Chapin Jr., then a Hudson sales executive (and a future chairman of American Motors), explained the situation this way: "If you don't have enough money to do something and do it right, and if you haven't learned to specialize in a given thing...sooner or later you find you just can't do everything. [Hudson was] usually reacting, rather than anticipating."

Nevertheless, Hudson had a fine 1950, selling another 143,586 Step-Downs, including more than 60,000 Pacemakers and Pacemaker Deluxes. Generally priced under $2000, the standard Pacemaker carried a destroked version of Hudson's new 1948 flathead "Super Six," sized at 232 cubic inches (bore and stroke: 3.56 × 3.88 inches). Though horsepower was only 112, performance was as good as that of Nash's top-line Ambassador, and well ahead of most comparably priced rivals. Back from 1948-49 were four "senior" series on a 124-inch wheelbase. The Super Six and Commodore Six used a 262-cid "stroker" (3.56 × 4.38) with 123 bhp; it also powered Pacemaker Deluxes. The Super Eight and Commodore Eight retained an elderly long-stroke inline flathead with 254 cid (3.00 × 4.50) and 128 bhp.

Pacemakers and Super Sixes came as fastback four-door sedans, long-deck club coupes, and as convertibles and fastback two-door sedans called Brougham. There was also a three-passenger standard Pacemaker coupe, the 1950 price leader at $1807. Commodores deleted fastback two-doors, Super Eight the convertible. The main appearance change that year involved adding twin diagonal grille bars—Hudson's familiar triangle motif.

All 1950 Hudsons offered optional overdrive ($95), Drive-Master ($105), or Supermatic Drive ($199). The latter two were semi-automatics. Drive-Master eliminated both shifting and clutching; you started off in "High" range, though in low gear, then let up on the accelerator to select second when desired. Supermatic, which added a high cruising ratio, shifted to second automatically at 22 mph if a dashboard button was engaged. Of course, neither was a substitute for full automatic transmission, which arrived for 1951 in the form of GM Hydra-Matic at only $158 (at which time Supermatic was dropped).

But Hudson's big '51 news was the powerful six-cylinder Hornet, a four-model line priced the same as Commodore Eight ($2540-$3100). At 308 cubic inches (3.81 × 4.50), the Hornet engine was one of the biggest production sixes ever, and though it made just 145 bhp initially, it was capable of far more in the hands of precision tuners.

Undoubtedly the most famous Hudson wrenchspinner was Marshall Teague, who claimed he could get 112 mph from an AAA- or NASCAR-certified stock Hornet. An enthusiastic cadre of Hudson engineers helped by conjuring a raft of "severe usage" options—actually thinly disguised racing parts. By late 1953 they'd even cooked up a hot "7-X" racing engine with about 210 bhp via 0.020 overbored cylinders, special cam and head, larger valves, higher compression, and "Twin-H Power" (dual carbs and manifolds—the first twin manifolds on a six).

The Hornet proved a near-invincible stock-car racer in 1951-54. Teague finished his 1952 AAA season with a 1000-point lead over his closest rival after winning 12 of the 13 scheduled events. Meantime, NASCAR aces Herb Thomas, Dick Rathmann, Al Keller, and Frank Mundy drove Hornets to 27 victories in 1952, another 21 in 1953, and 17 in 1954. Usually, three out of every four Hornets finished the races they entered. Hornets kept on winning after '54, when the Step-Down gave way to Nash-based "Hash" models.

But racing success effected little change on production Hudsons, and sales declined accordingly. Though the company kept adding and subtracting series through 1954, it couldn't alter styling much, nor add any new body styles after the Hollywood hardtop coupe bowed for 1951 in Hornet, Super Six, and Commodore Six/Eight form. The Super Eight and standard Pacemaker disappeared that year. Remaining models were facelifted with more massive, full-width grilles; larger rear windows also graced non-hardtop closed models.

More trim was shuffled for '52, when Super Six was renamed Wasp and gained a slightly more potent 127-bhp 262 engine, shared with the Commodore Six. Commodores were cut entirely for '53, leaving 119-inch-wheelbase Wasp coupe and sedans, the same plus Hollywood and convertible in new upmarket Super Wasp trim, and the four Hornets on the 124-inch platform. One bright spot: The Hornet six now delivered 15 extra bhp, and the 170-bhp 7-X engine was a regular factory option.

But Step-Down production diminished in each of these years, falling from 92,859 for '51 to exactly 70,000, then to

1951 Hudson Hornet Hollywood hardtop coupe

1953 Hudson Hornet four-door sedan

1954 Hudson Italia coupe

1954 Hudson Super Jet Club Sedan

1955 Hudson Wasp Custom four-door sedan

1956 Hudson Hornet 6 Custom four-door sedan

45,000 for 1953. Though government-ordered Korean War production cutbacks didn't help, military contracts earned Hudson an $8.3 million profit in 1952. Alas, that was more than wiped out by staggering 1953 losses totaling over $10.4 million.

That partly reflected the $12 million bill for Hudson's first compact, the ill-fated Jet, which arrived that year. Offered as a standard-trim notchback four-door and nicer "Super Jet" two- and four-door models, the Jet carried a 202-cid inline six (3.00 × 4.75) carved from the old Commodore eight. Only 104 bhp was standard, but optional "Twin-H" Power and high-compression head delivered 112 bhp, which made the little 105-inch-wheelbase Hudsons fairly speedy. Jets were also roadable and well-built, but not very pretty. Over the objections of chief designer Frank Spring (who'd shaped the Step-Down in wartime doodles), Hudson managers, led by the conservative A.E. Barit, insisted on bolt-upright, slab-sided styling that failed to impress. Hudson tried harder for 1954, adding a very cheap Family Club sedan ($1621) and luxurious Jet-Liners (around $2050), but sales went from

1953's bad (21,143) to worse (14,224).

However, the Jet sparked a project that might have become the much-needed Step-Down replacement. Called Italia, this was a four-place gran turismo designed by Spring and bodied on the Jet chassis by Carrozzeria Touring of Milan. Features included wrapped windshield, doors cut into the roof, fender scoops that channeled cooling air to the brakes, flow-through ventilation, form-fitting leather seats, and a 10-inch lower stance than production '54 Step-Downs. But with the 114-bhp Jet engine, Italias weren't very fast, and their aluminum bodywork wasn't very solid. Still, these problems might have been solved if Hudson had the money, which it didn't. As a result, Touring built only 25 "production" Italias, plus the prototype and a four-door derivative called X-161 (the would-be '55 Hudson). Project sales manager Roy Chapin, Jr. shoved Italias out the door as fast as he could at $4800 a copy. "I got rid of them," he said, "[but] it wasn't one of my greatest accomplishments."

Nor, for that matter, was the last-gasp Step-Down of 1954. Somehow, Hudson found money for a one-piece

1957 Hudson Hornet Custom four-door sedan

windshield and a below-the-belt reskin that imparted fashionable GM squareness—and an unfortunate resemblance to the dumpy Jet. Cheap Hornet Specials—club coupe and two fastback sedans—were added at around $2600, but the Step-Down was just too old to sell anymore. Model-year production totaled 36,436.

The '54 Hudsons bowed amid rumors of a Hudson-Nash merger. The talk was true, and Nash couldn't have come calling at a better time. From January 1, 1954 to its demise as an independent company in April, Hudson lost over $6 million on sales of just $28.7 million. However, Nash president George Mason insisted on one condition: The Jet had to go. Hudson's Barit resisted, but not for long. He was in no position to bargain.

The merger amounted to a Nash takeover. Mason hoped to add just-married Studebaker and Packard to this new American Motors Corporation, but that was doomed by his untimely death, thus ending his dream of a "Big Fourth" automaker.

With George Romney succeeding Mason as AMC president, Hudson's Detroit plant was closed and production transferred to Nash's hometown of Kenosha, Wisconsin. In late '54 came an "all-new" '55 Hudson, but everyone knew what it was: a restyled Nash. This wasn't all bad. Hudson could not only again tout unit-construction but Nash's all-coil suspension, plus lighter, trimmer cars that promised better economy.

And AMC stylists hid the Nash origins well, giving Hudsons a handsome eggcrate grille, distinct trim, a different rear end, full front-wheel openings (instead of semi-skirted), plus Nash's new '55 wrapped windshield. One direct link to previous Hudsons: 1954 gauges.

Offerings began with Wasp Super and Custom sedans and Custom Hollywood hardtop with 114.3-inch Nash Statesman wheelbase and a 202 "Hi-Torque" six from the now-departed Jet. Hornet Six rode Nash's 121.3-inch Ambassador platform and offered the same three models with 160/170-bhp 308 engines. Topping the line were a trio of 208-bhp Hornet V-8s powered by a new 320-cid engine (3.81 × 3.50) purchased from Packard. Twin-H Power was again available for sixes, and Hudson-badged Nash Metropolitans and Ramblers were added to give Hudson dealers broader market coverage. Yet for all this—and a banner Detroit sales year—big-Hudson volume continued to wither: down to just 20,331.

Fewer models and horrendous "V-Line Styling" arrived for '56. AMC design chief Edmund E. Anderson gets blamed for the ugliest Hudsons in a generation. The Hornet Six was otherwise unchanged, but the Wasp was down to a lone four-door, and Hornet V-8s were replaced in March by downpriced Hornet Specials with AMC's own new 250-cid V-8 (3.50 × 3.25)—which had only 190 bhp. An anemic engine and terrible looks only depressed demand, and AMC built just 10,671 non-Rambler '56 Hudsons.

Styling didn't improve for '57, but horsepower did. The AMC V-8 was newly bored to 327 cid (4.00 × 3.25), netting a more respectable 255 bhp for a four-Hudson line of Hornet Super and Custom sedans and Hollywoods. But buyers had long since branded Hudson a loser, and all but 3876 stayed away in '57. With that, Hudson was put out of its misery at last, as was Nash. In their place for '58 was a new Rambler Ambassador line with much cleaner styling originally intended for Hudson and Nash.

In retrospect, dropping these venerable makes was just common sense. As Chapin later said: "...[T]he decision really was one that said we've got to spend our money and our effort and our concentration on the Rambler...." Thus expired two once-great names, with Hudson perhaps the greater, sadder loss. Given the Hornet's great performance record and the Step-Down's engineering legacy, one can only guess what Hudson might have become had things been different.

HUDSON AT A GLANCE										
Model Year	1950	1951	1952	1953	1954	1955	1956	1957	1958	1959
Price Range, $	1806-2893	1964-3099	2116-3342	1858-3342	1621-4800	1445-4800	1672-3159	2821-3101		
Weight Range, Lbs.	3445-3865	3380-3800	3305-3770	2650-3760	2635-3800	1803-3878	2891-3826	3631-3693		
Wheelbases, Ins.	119, 124	119, 124	119, 124	105-124	105-124	108-121.3	108-121.3	121.3		
6 Cyl. Engines, BHP	112, 123	112-145	112-145	104-145	104-160	90-170	120, 170			
8 Cyl. Engines, BHP	128	128	128			208	190, 208	255		

Imperial became a distinct make for 1955, and would remain so for the next two decades. Of course, the name had been used since the late Twenties to denote the most luxurious Chryslers—and that would prove a problem. Somehow, Imperial could never shake its image as a Chrysler, and this more than any other handicap limited sales in the prestige-conscious luxury field.

Nevertheless, the non-Chrysler Imperial enjoyed some of its best years in the Fifties. The beautiful '55 models, based extensively on Virgil Exner's earlier Parade Phaeton show cars and the Ghia-built Chrysler K-310 experimental, are widely regarded as the most desirable Imperials of all. Elegantly trimmed inside and out, these big 130-inch-wheelbase sedans and Newport hardtop coupes wore a distinctive split grille, unique "gunsight" taillights, modestly wrapped windshield, and circular rear wheel openings, making them among the best-looking of Chrysler Corporation's all-new '55 fleet. Chrome was abundant but tastefully applied; two-toning was limited to the roof.

Naturally, the '55s retained the brilliant Chrysler hemi-head V-8, still at 331 cubic inches (bore and stroke: 3.81 × 3.63 inches). Rated at 250 horsepower for this application (on 8.5:1 compression), it mated to the firm's new fully automatic two-speed PowerFlite transmission, first offered on '54 Imperials but now controlled by a slim chrome wand extending from the dash, rather than a column lever. At nearly 11,500 units for the model year, the newly distinct Imperial scored about double the volume of the last Chrysler Imperial, an auspicious beginning even though Cadillac's '55 output was 10 times as great, Lincoln's five times as high.

Wheelbase was stretched three inches for the '56 models, which made them the longest in that dimension. (It shrank to 129 inches thereafter.) The Newport was renamed Southampton and gained a four-door companion. Rear fenders, still topped by "gunsights," were raised into fins, but no '56 Chrysler product wore more attractive ones. Frontal styling was unchanged. Following Chrysler, the Hemi was bored to 354 cid (3.94 × 3.63) for a gain of 30 bhp (helped by 9.0:1 compression), and the PowerFlite gained pushbutton control, which would feature on Chrysler automatics through 1963. Though not as quick as a Chrysler 300, the 1955-56 Imperials were lively performers, yet surprisingly economical, winning luxury-class laurels in the Mobilgas Economy Runs of these years. The only significant option was air conditioning, priced at $567. List prices ranged from the mid-$4000s to just over $5000.

Also available in 1955-56 were long-wheelbase Crown Imperial sedans and limousines. Built in Detroit, these took over for the long eight-seat Dodge, DeSoto, and Chrysler sedans offered through '54. Styling and engineering followed that of standard Imperials, but Crown prices were much higher—$7100-$7700—and availability far more limited. Just 172 were built for '55, another 226 for '56. Reflecting the industry's general decline from record-setting '55, Imperial's total '56 volume dropped to just below 11,000 units.

Imperial was all-new for 1957, bearing second-genera-

1955 Imperial four-door sedan

1955 Imperial Newport hardtop coupe

1956 Imperial four-door sedan

1956 Imperial four-door sedan

tion "Forward Look" styling from design chief Exner, marked by huge tailfins (with vestigial gunsights in the trailing edges), airier rooflines with curved side glass (an industry first), a finely checked full-width grille, and, where law allowed, quad headlamps (in lieu of conventional dual units where state law didn't allow). Seeking higher sales, Imperial expanded from one series to three, adding more elaborately trimmed Crown and LeBaron versions of the standard pillared sedan and Southampton hardtops. The Crown also offered the line's only convertible—the first soft-top Imperial since 1951. LeBaron, named for the famed prewar coachworks closely associat-

1957 Imperial Crown Southampton hardtop sedan

1958 Imperial Crown Southampton hardtop coupe

1959 Imperial Crown Southampton hardtop coupe

ed with Chrysler, arrived in January 1957 as a pillared sedan and four-door Southampton. Both new series were priced considerably higher than standard offerings: $5400-$5600 for Crown, $5743 for either LeBaron.

All '57 Imperials came with Chrysler's superb new three-speed TorqueFlite automatic transmission and a Hemi enlarged to 392 cid (4.00×3.90), good for 325 bhp with 9.25:1 compression. Also shared with other Chrysler

products that year was torsion-bar front suspension that made for fine roadability—the best in the luxury field. With all this, Imperial showed surprising sales strength. Volume more than tripled from '56, reaching near 38,000 units. That was still far behind Cadillac's 122,000 but enough to better Lincoln, though the difference was less than 1500.

Though the Crown Imperial sedan vanished for '57, the limo returned with a breathtaking $15,075 base price, but that only reflected the fact that it was now built by Ghia of Turin, Italy. With such low sales, Chrysler could no longer justify the time and space necessary to build such cars, especially with projected tooling costs of some $3.3 million.

Each Ghia Crown limo began with an unfinished two-door hardtop body mounted on the more rigid convertible chassis, shipped to Turin with all body panels intact. Ghia cut the car apart, added 20.5 inches to wheelbase, reworked structure above the beltline, fitted and trimmed the luxurious interior, and finished off the exterior using 150 pounds of lead filler. Construction of each car took a month, and initial delays made the Crown Imperial a very late '57 introduction. Sales were not impressive: only 132 Ghia Crowns would be built by the time this line ended in 1965, but all were impeccably tailored. Exactly 36 were built to '57 specifications, followed by 31 of the '58s and only seven for '59.

A predictably minor facelift was ordained for the volume '58 Imperials. The main differences were circular parking lights (replacing rectangular), quad headlamps (now legal nationwide), and a simpler grille composed of fine horizontal segments. Prices were marginally higher across an unchanged lineup, and the 392 Hemi was booted to 345 bhp via another compression increase (to 10:1). Reflecting Exner's fondness for "Classic" styling themes was an optional round decklid hump suggesting a spare tire, a '57 option that continued to find favor in '58. But this proved to be a poor year for Chrysler in general, and only 16,133 Imperials were built. Imperial would again outsell Lincoln in 1959 and '60, but would never do so again. To the frustration of dealers, people still thought of these cars as "Chrysler Imperials"—and "Chrysler" had nowhere near the charisma of "Cadillac."

For 1959 came a more extensive facelift of Imperial's '57 styling, highlighted—for some, anyway—by a toothy grille and broad brushed-finish appliques on the lower rear flanks. For the first time, the standard series had a name—Custom—but the lineup was again unchanged. As at other Highland Park divisions, Imperial switched from Hemi to wedge-head V-8s: a new 350-bhp 413-cid unit (4.18×3.75) shared with '59 Chrysler New Yorkers. It provided comparable performance, but was more economical to build and maintain. Production inched up to some 17,270.

After 1960, Imperial was strictly an also-ran among the Big Three's luxury makes, though it built some fine cars. As ever, Cadillac was the overwhelming sales leader, Lincoln a distant second, and Imperial an even more distant third.

IMPERIAL AT A GLANCE					
Model Year	**1955**	**1956**	**1957**	**1958**	**1959**
Price Range, $	4483-7095	4832-7731	4736-15,075	4839-15,075	4910-15,075
Weight Range, Lbs.	4490-5230	4555-5205	4640-5960	4590-5960	4675-149.5
Wheelbases, Ins.	130, 149.5	133, 149.5	129, 149.5	129, 149.5	129, 149.5
6 Cyl. Engines, BHP	250	280	325	325, 345	325, 350

The Kaiser story through 1950 is also the Frazer story told earlier in these pages. Save styling details and the Kaiser's lesser furnishings and lower prices, the cars were the same: "Dutch" Darrin's roomy flush-fender sedan with 123.5-inch wheelbase and a "stroker" six of 226 cubic inches (bore and stroke: 3.31 × 4.38 inches) and 100/112 horsepower. Kaiser was the better seller, and those sales were good: 70,474 of the '47s and 91,821 of the '48s. Most were the basic Special model that cost some $350 less than the more opulent Custom. All told, young Kaiser-Frazer Corporation made a healthy $30 million on 1947-48 volume that put it ninth in Detroit production. No wonder it was called "the postwar wonder company."

Then came 1949, when chairman Henry Kaiser boldly tooled for 200,000 cars against the advice of his market-wise partner. K-F president Joe Frazer knew his company couldn't sell 200,000 cars against all-new 1949 Big Three competition. But Henry was undaunted, ordering up glittery facelifts as well as convertible sedans and Virginian

"hardtops" for the Kaiser Deluxe line (replacing Custom), plus clever Special Traveler and Deluxe Vagabond utility sedans with double-hatch rear and fold-down back seats. Despite all this, K-F's 1949 sales weren't even half what Henry planned, forcing about 26 percent of the some 95,000 Kaisers built to be reserialed for sale as "1950" models. By 1951, both Joe Frazer and the car named for him were gone.

Meantime, Darrin and K-F Styling had prepared a real blockbuster: a slender, beautiful new Kaiser with "Anatomic Design." Though scheduled for 1950, it didn't arrive until March of that year as a '51 offering (delayed until '49 leftovers were cleared). But it sold like no Kaiser before: close to 140,000 for the model year. From 17th in Detroit for '49, Kaiser promptly shot up to 12th—the highest it would ever go.

Looking unlike any other car of its day, the '51 Kaiser boasted 700 square inches more glass area than the nearest competitor and a lower beltline than any Detroit car

1951 Kaiser Special two-door sedan

1951 Kaiser DeLuxe four-door sedan

1951 Kaiser Special Traveler two-door sedan

1952 Kaiser Manhattan four-door sedan

1952 Kaiser Manhattan four-door sedan

1953 Kaiser Manhattan two-door sedan

1953 Kaiser "Hardtop" Dragon four-door sedan

1954 Kaiser Manhattan four-door sedan

1954 Kaiser Darrin roadster

1954 Kaiser Darrin roadster

1954 Kaiser Special four-door sedan

1955 Kaiser Manhattan four-door sedan

offered through 1956. Though wheelbase was trimmed to 118.5 inches, the '51 looked miles sleeker. Complementing its artful styling was a bewildering array of bright exterior colors and high-fashion interior trims, the work of K-F "color engineer" Carleton Spencer.

The '51 Kaiser was also the first car that actually sold at least partly on safety, offering a padded dash, recessed instruments, slim roof pillars for outstanding visibility, and a windshield that popped out if struck with a force of more than 35 pounds per square inch. Though chief engineers John Widman and Ralph Isbrandt shunned unit construction, they designed a very rigid separate body for a strong frame weighing but 200 pounds. They also provided a low center of gravity that ensured fine handling, and a suspension that delivered a terrific ride despite curb weights averaging only some 3100 pounds. Said a Chrysler engineer who later sampled a '51 Kaiser: "It rides like one of our 4500-pound cars." Interiors provided ample room for people of all sizes, hence the "Anatomic" moniker.

Still in the lower medium-price field, Kaiser's '51 prices ranged from just under $2000 to a bit over $2400. Special and Deluxe series returned, each offering regular and utility Traveler sedans with two or four doors, plus long-deck club coupe; there was also a stripped Special business coupe. But hardtops, convertibles, and station wagons were conspicuously absent, as was a V-8. Though K-F had plans for all of these, it would never have the money to market them. The old six was lifted to 115 bhp via two-barrel carburetor and dual exhausts, but the missing V-8 would prove an increasing sales liability.

A scheduled 1952 facelift wasn't quite ready on time, so Virginian models, basically leftover '51s with "Continental kit," were sold in the interim—about 5500 in all. The "real" '52s arrived with bulbous taillights and a more prominent, heavier-looking grille. Two-door Travelers and the business coupe departed, Specials became Deluxes, and upper models—a coupe and two sedans—were called Manhattan (borrowing an old Frazer name). The "second-series" '52s are fairly rare: only 7500 Deluxes and 19,000 Manhattans were produced.

Kaiser had pitched the "fashion market" in 1951 with its $125 Dragon trim options: limited-edition four-door sedans available in Golden, Silver, Emerald, and Jade editions. All sported alligator-look "Dragon" vinyl inside and color-keyed exteriors with padded vinyl tops. This idea was revived for 1953 with a "Hardtop" Dragon sedan, the most luxurious Kaiser of all. It was easily spotted by a gold-plated hood ornament, badges, and even keyhole covers, plus a padded roof usually covered in "bambu" vinyl, a tough, oriental-style material that also adorned the dash and parts of seats and door panels. Seat inserts were done in "Laguna" cloth, a fabric with an oblong pattern created by fashion designer Marie Nichols. Standard amenities were plentiful: tinted glass, Hydra-Matic Drive, whitewalls, twin-speaker radio, and Calpoint custom carpet. The finishing touch was a gold-plated dash plaque engraved with the owner's name. The Dragon was spectacular, but a high $3924 price—nearly as much as a Cadillac Coupe de Ville—limited sales to just 1277, and a few of those almost had to be given away.

Otherwise, the '53 Kaisers were little changed. A pair of stripped Carolina sedans was fielded in the $2300 range, an effort to build showroom traffic, but sold fewer than 1200. Club coupes were eliminated, the old six was tweaked to 118 bhp, and power steering bowed late in the season as a $122 option.

But Kaiser sales were falling fast: only 32,000 for '52 and just 28,000 for '53. The Henry J compact had squandered development funds that K-F would have better spent on new styling or a V-8. Cash reserves were further depleted in 1954, when Henry Kaiser decided to buy Willys-Overland, which was no better off.

Seeking to slash overhead, Kaiser transferred production from its huge Willow Run, Michigan plant to W-O's Toledo, Ohio facilities, and hoped for a sales miracle with a clever facelift by stylist "Buzz" Grisinger. From the front, the '54 Kaisers looked much like the Buick XP-300 show car (a favorite of company president Edgar Kaiser), with a wide, concave grille, dummy hood scoop, and headlights "floating" within oval housings. Out back were "Safety-Glo" taillights: the existing units given little finned housings with a lighted strip run forward atop the fenders.

Remaining Travelers were canceled for '54, but Manhattans were booted to a maximum 140 bhp by bolting on a McCulloch centrifugal supercharger that cut in at full throttle. Also offered that year were unsupercharged Specials in two "series." The first involved '53 Manhattans warmed-over with '54 front ends—yet another effort to use up leftovers. Second-series Specials were genuine '54s with wrapped rear windows, as on all of that year's Manhattans.

But sales refused to improve, and 1954 Kaiser production was a dismal 8539, including 4110 Manhattans, 3500 "early" Specials, and a paltry 929 "late" Specials. Accordingly, only Manhattans returned for '55, distinguished by a higher fin on the hood scoop and little else. Just 270 were sold. Another 1021 were exported, most to Argentina, where Kaiser Motors hoped to continue production at a subsidiary plant for South America. It's a tribute to the durability of this basic design that the '55 was built there through 1962 as the little-altered Kaiser Carabella.

A memorable last-gasp U.S. effort was the 1954 Kaiser-Darrin sliding-door sports car. Dutch designed it in late 1952 around the 100-inch-wheelbase Henry J chassis, and talked Henry Kaiser into selling it for $3668. Only 435 were built before Kaiser ceased U.S. production.

The Darrin was beautifully styled, and still looks good today. Besides a then-novel fiberglass body and the unique sliding doors, it boasted a three-way landau top with intermediate half-up position, plus full instrumentation and usually a three-speed floorshift transmission with overdrive. This plus the 90 bhp of the Henry J's 161-cid Willys six gave economy of around 30 mpg, but also 0-60 sprints of about 13 seconds and near-100 mph flat out.

But the Kaiser-Darrin affair greatly disappointed Dutch, who bought about 100 leftovers, fitted many with Cadillac V-8s, and sold them for $4350 apiece at his Los Angeles showroom. The V-8 Darrins were potent indeed, capable of some 140 mph.

Kaiser came to an end in America during 1955 after 10 years and $100 million in losses. They were usually good cars and often innovative, but they never grabbed the attention of the public. Edgar Kaiser liked to say, "Slap a Buick nameplate on it and it would sell like hotcakes." He was probably right.

KAISER AT A GLANCE						
Model Year	**1950**	**1951**	**1952**	**1953**	**1954**	**1955**
Price Range, $	1995-2288	1992-2433	1992-2759	2313-3924	2334-3668	2617-2670
Weight Range, Lbs.	3311-3726	3106-3345	3110-3310	3135-3435	2175-3375	3335-3375
Wheelbases, Ins.	123.5	118.5	118.5	118.5	100, 118.5	118.5
6 Cyl. Engines, BHP	100-112	115	115	118	90-140	140

Lincoln was founded to build World War I Liberty aero engines by Henry Martyn Leland, the "master of precision" who had started Cadillac, made it "Standard of the World," and counted "Honest Abe" among his heroes. With son Wilfred, Leland then turned Lincoln to "precision-built" cars, but encountered financial problems and was bought out by Henry Ford in 1922. By the early Thirties, guided by Ford's artistic son Edsel, Lincoln rose to rival Cadillac and Packard with its magnificently styled K-series V-12s. But like other luxury makes, Lincoln survived the Depression mainly with medium-priced cars: the streamlined, unitized Zephyr that also spawned the 1940-41 Continental, one of motoring's all-time great designs.

Yet this distinguished heritage was just so much old news as Lincoln entered the Fifties with continuations of its all-new 1949 models. Like the first all-postwar Packard, Hudson, and Nash, their styling was of the bulbous "inverted bathtub" school, with a look evolved from occasional work during World War II by the Bob Gregorie design offices at Ford. Though Lincolns were easily distinguished by their sunken headlamps (covers were originally intended), they appeared little more than big Mercurys—which wasn't quite true. Cosmopolitan, the upper Lincoln line of this period, rode a 125-inch wheelbase and shared no body panels with Mercury, though the 121-inch-wheelbase standard Lincolns share Mercury's bodyshell from the cowl back.

The explanation lies in Ford's postwar planning. What became the production 118-inch-wheelbase Mercury was originally slated as the '49 Ford; the eventual standard Lincoln was planned as the '49 Mercury. But at the last minute, Ford's Policy Committee, led by Ernest R. Breech and chief engineer Harold Youngren, decreed a new 114-inch-wheelbase design for the '49 Ford, so the original Ford and Mercury were moved up to become the '49 Mercury and standard Lincoln, and a planned '49 Zephyr survived as the Cosmopolitan. The ex-Mercury Lincolns were thus much cheaper than the Cosmos, spanning a $2500-$3100 range versus $3200-$3950. A stillborn casualty of the 11th-hour model realignment was a new postwar Continental, though that would emerge for 1956 as the very different Mark II (see "Continental").

Lincoln's 1950 line was slightly changed from '49. The standard series lost a convertible, while Cosmo deleted a fat-looking fastback four-door, the oddly named Town Sedan. This left a notchback coupe and four-portal Sport Sedan (with throwback "suicide" rear doors) in each series, plus Cosmo convertible. There were also two newcomers, the $2721 Lido and $3406 Cosmopolitan Capri. Both were limited-edition coupes with custom interiors and padded canvas tops, offered in lieu of a true pillarless hardtop like Cadillac's Coupe de Ville. Few were sold through 1951.

Also new for 1950 was a dashboard restyled by chief designer Tom Hibbard: an attractive rolled affair with oblong instrument cluster, a format that would persist through 1957. Hydra-Matic transmission, bought from archrival GM, arrived as a new option; it would be standard in 1952-54. Lincoln's 1950 powerplant remained as for '49: a 336.7 cubic-inch L-head V-8 (bore and stroke: 3.50 × 4.38 inches). Originally designed for Ford trucks, it made 152 horsepower, and would continue only through '51 (though with two horses more). That would also be the last year for the "bathtub" styling, which was slightly improved by longer rear fenders, upright taillamps (replacing round units), and a simpler grille.

While not known for performance, Lincoln had enough of the right stuff to place ninth in the 1950 *Carrera Panamericana*—the first of the now-legendary Mexican Road Races. Lincoln then won the 1951 Mobilgas Economy Run at an average 25.5 mpg. But neither of these feats helped 1950-51 sales, which were well down on 1949's record 73,500. The totals were a bit over 28,000 for 1950 and a more encouraging 32,500 for '51.

All Ford Motor Company cars were completely new for '52, none more than Lincoln. But though sales rose—to nearly 41,000 by '53—Lincoln was still miles behind Cadillac. One problem may have been the sedate squarish lines of this period—again very close to Mercury, but also Ford. Uniformity may have caused trouble too, with the same five models through 1954. Cosmopolitan now denoted the lower series, Capri the upper. Both listed four-door sedan and two-door hardtop (the latter arriving three years behind Cadillac's); Capri added a convertible.

Nevertheless, 1952-54 was a significant period in Lincoln history. The most notable mechanical development was the make's first overhead-valve V-8: a modern new short-stroke design of 317.5-cid (3.80 × 3.50), good for 160 bhp at first and 205 bhp for 1953-54. It was superior in many ways. Its crankshaft, for example, had eight counterweights versus most competitors' six. Intake valves were oversize for better breathing and higher specific output (among '53 engines it produced 0.64 bhp per cubic inch, versus 0.63 for Cadillac and 0.54 for the Chrysler Hemi.) The crankcase extended below the crankshaft centerline to form an extremely stiff shaft support, hence this engine's family nickname "Y-block."

Nineteen fifty-two also brought ball-joint front suspension to Lincoln. Together with the new V-8, it made for taut, powerful road machines that would dominate their class in the Mexican Road Race. Other new features included recirculating-ball power steering, oversize drum brakes, liberal sound insulation, optional four-way power seat and, with the extra-cost factory air conditioning, flow-through ventilation when the compressor was turned off. Fabrics and leathers, fit and finish were of a quality that far exceeded conventional Ford products.

Despite a rather short 123-inch wheelbase, the 1952-54 Lincolns were roomier inside than previous models—and some later ones. Visibility was better than on any other contemporary U.S. car save Kaiser, and exteriors were notably free of the era's excesses. Fluted taillights shed water and dirt just like those Mercedes would adopt in the late Seventies.

Lincoln turned in some spectacular performances at the *Carrera Panamericana*—virtually unrivalled in the International Standard Class. Lincolns took the first five

1950 Lincoln Cosmopolitan Sport Sedan four-door

1950 Lincoln Cosmopolitan Sport Sedan four-door

1951 Lincoln Cosmopolitan convertible coupe

1952 Lincoln Capri hardtop coupe

1953 Lincoln Capri convertible coupe

1954 Lincoln Capri four-door sedan

1954 Lincoln Capri convertible coupe

1955 Lincoln Capri hardtop coupe

places in 1952, the top four in '53, and first and second in 1954. Major credit for race preparation goes to Clay Smith, a gifted mechanic who was tragically killed in a pit accident in 1954. Of great help were publicity-conscious Dearborn engineers who supplied stiff "export" suspension components, Ford truck camshafts, mechanical valve lifters, special front spindles and hubs, and rear axle ratios that enabled a stock Lincoln to top 130 mph. The 1952 race winner, Chuck Stevenson, actually finished the 2000-mile grind from Juarez to the Guatemala border nearly an hour ahead of the Ferrari that had won the year before.

Lincoln wasn't ready with a total redesign for 1955, and its cars were among the most conservative in Detroit that year, this despite a heavy facelift. Still, styling was crisp, clean, and elegant. Though the wrapped windshield held sway most everywhere else, Lincoln didn't have one yet, and was thus more practical. Interiors remained luxurious combinations of quality fabrics and top-grain leather.

Wheelbase was naturally unchanged for '55, but the restyle added extra sheetmetal and 50-100 pounds in curb weight. A good thing, then, that the V-8 was bored to 3.94 inches for 341 cid and a useful 20 extra horsepower.

1956 Lincoln Premiere hardtop coupe

1956 Lincoln Premiere four-door sedan

Elsewhere, Cosmopolitan was retagged Custom, and Lincoln finally offered its own automatic transmission. Called Turbo-Drive, this was basically the four-year-old Ford/Merc-O-Matic unit enlarged and strengthened to withstand the greater torque of Lincoln's V-8. But likely because its '55s weren't "new" enough, Lincoln was one of the few makes to suffer a sales decline in Detroit's banner year of the decade, dropping from nearly 37,000 for '54 to a bit over 27,000.

The '56s *were* new—very new. Though ads proclaimed them "Unmistakably Lincoln," there was scarcely a trace of the trim '55s. Wheelbase grew three inches, overall length seven inches, width three inches. Capri now adorned the lower-priced series, Premiere the costlier one, but body-style assignments were unchanged, though pillared four-doors were made to look much like hardtops. Styling, partly previewed by the 1954 Mercury XM-800 show car, was fully up to date: wrapped windshield, clean grille, peaked headlights, simple ornamentation, two-toning confined to the roof, and rakish vertical taillights capping long exhaust ports on either side of a "grille" motif duplicating the front.

Lincoln's '56 V-8 was as expansive as its styling: enlarged to 368 cid (4.00 × 3.66) and 285 bhp—"True power," blared the ads, "that works for your safety at every speed." Despite their greater bulk, the '56s didn't weigh much more than the '55s. But they cost more: a whopping $500-$700, the range now running from $4120 to near $4750. Yet as the only make with a major restyle instead of a mere facelift for '56, Lincoln did well, moving over 50,000 cars. Still, even that was only about a third of Cadillac's total.

Prices rose another $500-$700 for 1957, when Lincoln joined a popular Detroit trend by offering its first four-door hardtop, dubbed "Landau," in both series. Huge tailfins sprouted, and the '56 front was modified with "Quadra-Lite" styling: conventional seven-inch-diameter headlamps above 5¾-inch "road" lamps; though not a true a four-light system, the look was a bit ahead of most competitors. Compression went to 10:1, yielding 300 bhp from the 368 V-8.

Overall, 1957 was a good, but not great, Lincoln year. At a bit over 41,000, model-year volume was slightly higher than Imperial's but only a fifth of Cadillac's. For 1958,

1957 Lincoln Premiere hardtop coupe

1957 Lincoln Premiere convertible coupe

1959 Lincoln Continental Mark IV convertible coupe

Lincoln pinned its hopes on yet another all-new design.

But '58 proved awful considering the millions invested in new tooling. The economy bottomed out and overall car sales fell 50 percent or more from '57 levels. Ford trailed Chevrolet by a quarter-million units, Edsel began its rapid slide to nowhere, and Mercury ran 40 percent behind its '57 sales pace. The new '58 Lincolns were longer, lower, and wider at a time when many buyers began thinking of more sensible dimensions. Model-year production duly tumbled to about 17,000.

At the bottom of this avalanche was a square-lined unibody giant on a 131-inch wheelbase stretching six inches longer overall than the '57 Lincoln. It was easily recognized, for there was nothing else like it: heavily sculptured sides, a wide grille flanked by true quad headlights in slanted recesses, gigantic flared bumpers. Under a hood not much smaller than a basketball court was 1958's largest American passenger-car engine: a new big-block 430-cid V-8 (4.30 × 3.70) making 375 bhp.

Of course, this package had been conceived in the far healthier market of 1955. And recession or not, most luxury buyers still wanted cars like this. Yet Cadillac attracted more customers with a heavy facelift, and Imperial garnered residual sales with its finned wonders. Both rivals had lately expanded their lineups, and comparable '58 Cadillacs were priced several hundred dollars below Lincolns. But if 1958 was a debacle for Dearborn's prestige make, it ushered in designer Elwood Engel and a three-year program that would culminate in a more compact— and vastly more successful—new Lincoln for 1961.

Meantime, there was nothing to do but offer more of the same, so both Lincolns and Continentals were little changed for '59. The Premiere convertible had been transferred to the related but ostensibly distinct 1958 Continental Mark III line, leaving six standard Lincolns: four-door sedan and two- and four-door hardtops, Capri, and Premiere. These returned for '59, when Continental was added as a Lincoln sub-series following the decision to combine Continental Division with Edsel and Lincoln-Mercury to form M-E-L Division (which with Edsel's demise would revert to plain L-M after this one year).

The '59 Mark IV was just a facelifted Mark III, but offered a new formal-roof Town Car and limousine priced about the same as the old $10,000 Mark II. Likewise, '59 Lincolns were lightly touched-up '58s with less horsepower (350 bhp, as on the Marks). Though the division desperately held prices close to previous levels—$4900-$5500 for Lincolns, $6600-$7000 for the standard Marks— Imperial surged ahead in 1959 model-year production— and would win again the following year. Lincoln's '59 total was dismal enough: 15,780.

But adversity often sows the seeds of success, and Lincoln would blossom anew in the Sixties. Nevertheless, most any Fifties Lincoln is now a prime collector's item. The "Road Race" 1952-54s found favor long ago, but "bathtubs," the '55s, and the expansive 1956-57s are fast-rising in esteem and values. Even the blocky giants of 1958-59—which handle far better than some latterday revisionists admit—now have their fans. Too bad they weren't around at the time.

LINCOLN AT A GLANCE										
Model Year	1950	1951	1952	1953	1954	1955	1956	1957	1958	1959
Price Range, $	2527-3948	2745-4234	3517-4025	3522-4031	3522-4031	3563-4072	4119-4747	4649-5381	4951-5565	4902-5594
Weight Range, Lbs.	3970-4490	4065-4615	4140-4350	4125-4350	4135-4310	4185-4415	4305-4452	4373-4676	4735-4880	4741-4887
Wheelbases, Ins.	121, 125	121, 125	123	123	123	123	126	126	131	131
8 Cyl. Engines, BHP	152	154	160	205	205	225	285	300	375	350

Mercury began the Fifties with continuations of its all-new "junior Lincolns" of 1949, then briefly returned to its usual role as "senior Ford" before finally becoming "its own car." Through all these transformations, one thing was constant: a "hot car" image that was a big sales asset, as it had been ever since Mercury was launched in 1939.

It was conceived largely by Edsel Ford, who saw a place for it some time before old father Henry did. At first, Mercury was a "super Ford": bigger, brighter, more deluxe, with a bigger flathead V-8 providing more power and better performance. The intent was to bridge the yawning price gap that then existed between Ford and Lincoln's medium-priced Zephyr, and Edsel carefully pitched Mercury against the eight-cylinder Pontiac but somewhat below Oldsmobile. Though Mercury didn't approach the volume of those GM makes, it averaged some 80,000 annual sales through the early Forties, running 12th-14th in the industry and bringing Dearborn important business that would otherwise have been lost to competitors. Mercury maintained this pace with its 1946-48 models, which like most other Detroiters were simply warmed-over '42s.

That the Mercury formula changed for 1949 was the accidental result of a last-minute model realignment for Dearborn's first all-postwar fleet. Wheelbase was unchanged—the same 118 inches used since 1941—but a new bodyshell shared with that year's standard Lincolns brought "inverted bathtub" styling of the sort favored by several automakers at the time. But that styling was good—clean, if massive—and would prove popular through 1951, helped by the customized "bathtub Merc" of smoldering teen movie star James Dean in *Rebel Without a Cause*.

The rest of Mercury's '49 package would also continue through '51, as would a basic four-model line of coupe, four-door Sport Sedan (with rear-hinged "suicide" back doors), convertible, and two-door wagon with structural woodwork. Like Fords, the '49 Mercurys boasted Dearborn's first fully independent front suspension, plus a modernized leaf-spring rear end. Resuming its power lead over Ford, Mercury swapped its former 239.4 cubic-inch flathead V-8 for a stroked 255.4-cid version (bore and stroke: 3.19 × 4.00), with dual-downdraft Holley carburetors. The result was 110 horsepower, up 10, and genuine 100-mph performance for the first time. Also introduced was an automatic overdrive option priced at $97, teamed with 4.27:1 rear axle instead of the normal 3.90:1.

The 1949 Mercury was an attractive buy with its Lincolnesque styling, lower prices ($1979-$2716), and more power than Ford (necessary to offset some 300 extra pounds in curb weight). Buyers responded by taking over 301,000 of the '49s—more than three times Mercury's previous best volume, and good for sixth in industry production, another all-time high.

Sales continued strong into the Fifties despite few changes: close to 294,000 for 1950 and a record-setting 310,000-plus for '51, when Mercury again claimed sixth. The '50s gained a hood-front chrome molding bearing the

1950 Mercury convertible coupe

1950 Mercury Monterey Club Coupe

Mercury name. The '51s combined this with a large semicircular crest; they also sported more prominent grille bars, larger parking lights (swept back to the front wheel wells), and longer rear fenders with rounded corners that dropped straight down. The '51s also gained a nominal two horsepower and, more significantly, optional Merc-O-Matic Drive, the new three-speed automatic transmission developed with the Warner Gear Division of Borg-Warner (and also offered that year as Ford-O-Matic by you-know-who).

A couple of new model variations were added for 1950: a stripped price-leader coupe ($1875) and the interesting Monterey. The latter was a spiffy limited edition with upgraded interior and a top covered in canvas or leather. At around $2150, the Monterey cost some $160 more than the standard coupe, but it wasn't the costliest 1950-51 Merc (the wagon was over $400 more). Its purpose, as with the concurrent Ford Crestliner and Lincoln Lido/Capri, was to stand in for the pillarless "hardtop-convertibles" being offered by GM and Chrysler rivals.

Hardtops arrived in force for 1952, when Ford Motor Company was the only Big Three producer with all-new styling. Mercury got a pair: Sport Coupe and a more deluxe Monterey version (*sans* covered roof). Monterey was also offered as a convertible and four-door sedan. Following an industry trend, wagons were now all-steel four-doors with simulated wood trim. Two- and four-door sedans (without "suicide" doors) again completed the line. Bodyshells again came from Ford, though Mercury retained a three-inch longer wheelbase, all of it ahead of the cowl. Also shared with Ford was 1952's tight, clean styling, though a resemblance to that year's new Lincoln didn't hurt. Higher compression boosted the flat-

1951 Mercury two-door station wagon

1953 Mercury Monterey four-door sedan

1952 Mercury Monterey convertible coupe

1954 Mercury Monterey Sun Valley hardtop coupe

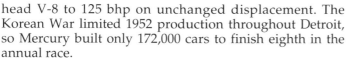

head V-8 to 125 bhp on unchanged displacement. The Korean War limited 1952 production throughout Detroit, so Mercury built only 172,000 cars to finish eighth in the annual race.

Mercury's first two-series line bowed for 1953: Custom hardtop and two- and four-door sedans; Monterey convertible, hardtop, wagon, and four-door sedan. Retained from '52 was a trendy dashboard with aircraft-type lever controls flanking a large half-moon gauge cluster. Business picked up with the end of Korean War restrictions, and Mercury moved nearly 305,000 cars, though it again ran eighth. Prices picked up, but only a little, ranging from $2000 for the Custom two-door to near $2600 for the Monterey wagon.

Nineteen fifty-four brought a significant engineering change in Mercury's first overhead-valve V-8, a bigger version of the new "Y-Block" design featured on that year's Ford. Though little larger than Mercury's previous L-head—256 cid—the ohv had modern short-stroke dimensions (3.62 × 3.10), five-main-bearing crankshaft, and much more horsepower: a rated 161 with standard four-barrel carburetor. With low 3.9:1 rear axle and standard transmission, it made the '54 Mercs very quick off the line. Equally noteworthy was ball-joint front suspension, another development shared with Ford.

Styling improved for '54 via wraparound taillights and a clean but more aggressive grille with larger bullet guards. Joining previous models was the top-line Sun Valley hardtop, which is more famous now than it was then. An outgrowth of Dearborn's experiments with plastic-topped cars (as was Ford's similar Skyliner), the Sun Valley was nice in theory: the airiness of a convertible combined with closed-car comfort and practicality. In practice, though, it was something else. Though the Plexiglas front half-roof was tinted, and a snap-in shade was provided for really hot weather, customers complained that the interior heated up like an oven. Predictably, sales weren't impressive: just 9761 of the '54s and a mere 1787 for '55.

At about 260,000 units in all, 1954 wasn't Mercury's greatest sales year, but hopes were high for '55. With a more potent V-8, colorful new styling on the basic 1952-54 shell, and the first wheelbase increase since '41—to 119 inches except for wagons, which remained at 118—the '55s couldn't miss. And they didn't: A record 329,000-plus were built.

Topping the '55 line was the new Montclair series of four-door sedan, hardtop, convertible, and Sun Valley—all bearing a thin contrast-color panel outlined in bright metal beneath the side windows. One step below were Monterey sedan, hardtop, and wagon, followed by the Custom series with the same body styles plus a two-door sedan. Mercury's first wrapped windshield, an evolutionary '54 grille, hooded headlamps, and eye-catching surface ornamentation were common to all. A Y-block V-8 swelled to 292 cid (3.75 × 3.30) arrived in two forms: 188 bhp for Custom and Monterey, 198 bhp for Montclair and as an option for lower series, available only with Merc-O-Matic.

Four-door Phaeton hardtops arrived for 1956's "Big M" line, which represented an ambitious expansion into somewhat uncharted territory. To stay competitive in the face of rising prices, Mercury fielded cut-rate Medalist models—two- and four-door hardtops and sedans—pitched at the bottom of the medium-price field. But inflation made these "low-priced" Mercs costlier than the pre-

1955 Mercury Montclair Sun Valley hardtop coupe

1956 Mercury Monterey Phaeton hardtop sedan

1956 Mercury Medalist hardtop coupe

1957 Mercury Commuter four-door hardtop station wagon

vious year's Customs ($2250-$2460), and not sufficiently cheaper than the better-trimmed 1956 Customs ($2350-$2800). Dealers pushed hard with two-door sedans, but only 45,812 of the '56 Medalists were sold. Custom, Monterey, and Montclair all outsold the price-leader by at least 2-1. Medalist was duly dropped, only to resurface for '58 in a price segment once meant for the new Edsel.

Mercury's '56 styling was a good update of its '55 look. All models save Medalists wore bold "Z-line" side trim that delineated the contrast color area with optional two-toning (the area below was generally matched to the roof). In the Monterey and Montclair lines, the Phaeton hardtop sedans were mid-season replacements for low-roof pillared Sport Sedans, a holdover style from mid-1955. Mercury also offered a second convertible for the first time, in the Custom group. The Y-block was enlarged

again, this time to 312 cid (3.80 × 3.44), good for 210-235 bhp, the latter standard for Monterey and Montclair.

Though 1956 was a downbeat year for the industry as a whole, Mercury was an exception, rolling out some 328,000 cars, only a bit off its '55 pace. An encouraging sign was that the premium Montclair managed to sell almost as well as the year before. The mid-line Monterey was still the breadwinner, though.

The '57s were all-new, trumpeted as "a dramatic expression of dream car design." They were: inspired (really previewed) by the XM-Turnpike Cruiser show car of 1956, which also had direct showroom counterparts in new top-line Turnpike Cruiser two- and four-door hardtops. Glitz and gimmicks were standard: "skylight dual curve windshield," drop-down reverse-slant rear window, dual air intakes over the A-posts housing little horizontal antennae. If that wasn't enough, you could order the creatively named "Seat-O-Matic," which automatically powered the front seat to one of 49 possible positions at the twist of two dials. Mercury also joined Chrysler in offering pushbutton automatic transmission controls for '57. Arriving late in the season was a Convertible Cruiser, honoring Mercury's selection as '57 Indy 500 pace car, and supplied with similar regalia decals. Yet for all their gadgetry (or maybe because of it) the Cruisers failed miserably. They were not just expensive—$3760-$3850 for the hardtops, $4100 for the ragtop—but too far out even for that gilded age.

Nineteen fifty-seven's major redesign gave Mercury its own bodyshells and a new 122-inch-wheelbase chassis—the first time it was neither senior Ford nor junior Lincoln.

1957 Mercury Turnpike Cruiser hardtop coupe

1958 Mercury Montclair convertible coupe

1959 Mercury Park Lane hardtop coupe

A minor facelift yielded slightly quieter styling for 1958, but the year was a disaster, production falling to 153,000. The Convertible Cruiser was abandoned (after only 1265 of the '57s) and the two hardtops became Montclair sub-models. Lower prices failed to perk up sales (barely 6400 between them). The cheap Medalist returned for a short encore with two- and four-door sedans, but again proved disappointing: only 18,732 sales. Topping the line was the new Park Lane group of two hardtops and a convertible (also offered as Montclairs and Montereys), ostensible Cruiser replacements with less hokum and Lincoln's new 430 V-8 (4.30 × 3.70) with 360 bhp. A smooth three-speed automatic called Multi-Drive debuted (basically Ford Division's new Cruise-O-Matic), as did a 383 V-8—same displacement as Chrysler's engine but with more over-square dimensions (4.30 × 3.30). Standard for all '58 Mercs save Park Lane and Medalist (which came with a 235-bhp 312), the 383 delivered 312 or 330 bhp.

Though the bottom dropped out of the medium-price market in '58, Mercury remained eighth despite building only 40 percent of its '57 volume. But significantly, the compact Rambler passed the Big M in sales and took out after Pontiac, Olds, and Buick. Mercury would join the swing to compacts and intermediates soon enough. In the meantime, it could only offer more of the same.

More the '59 Mercurys definitely had, with even bigger bodies on a new 126-inch wheelbase. Styling was still square but more sculptured, marked by a mile-wide grille, huge bumpers at each end, enormous windshields and rear windows, and a more sharply creased version of the odd 1957-58 rear fender motif. Medalist and Turnpike Cruiser were forgotten, and two of the four remaining series were severely cropped, Montclair and wagons each going from six models to four. Engines were detuned as a sop to a newly economy-conscious public. The lineup comprised 210- and optional 280-bhp 312s for Monterey, a 345-bhp 430 for Park Lane, and 280- and 322-bhp 383s for other models. Yet despite this retrenchment, Mercury's '59 volume failed to top 150,000 units.

In retrospect, Mercury sales stumbled after 1956 at least in part because the fleet, good-looking cars of earlier years were replaced by shiny, begadgeted behemoths that couldn't hope to sell well in a down economy. But the division would find its way back to "hot cars" in the Sixties and, with them, new success.

Like the all-new '57 Ford, this was done partly to prepare for the '58 Edsel line, which borrowed some from both makes. Monterey and Montclair were bereft of station wagons, which were now a separate series with no fewer than six models: from the top, woody-look Colony Park, a four-door nine-seater; plain-sided two- and four-door Voyagers; and three Commuters with the various seat and door combinations. All had pillarless hardtop styling.

All the '57 Big Ms looked a bit heavy and quite contrived, with massive dual-oblong bumpers, available quad headlights (where legal, regular duals otherwise), and long scallops in the upper rear fenders leading to pie-slice taillamps. A 255-bhp 312 V-8 was standard except on Cruisers, which had a 290-bhp 368-cid Lincoln engine.

Mercury did fairly well for '57, but not as well as in '56. Volume dropped to a bit over 286,000 and the make's production rank from seventh to eighth—not encouraging for an all-new design in a fairly strong sales year.

MERCURY AT A GLANCE										
Model Year	**1950**	**1951**	**1952**	**1953**	**1954**	**1955**	**1956**	**1957**	**1958**	**1959**
Price Range, $	1875-2560	2189-2759	2191-2834	2194-2826	2194-2776	2218-2844	2254-2977	2576-4103	2547-4118	2768-4206
Weight Range, Lbs.	3321-3626	3485-3800	3335-3795	3335-3795	3435-3735	3450-3780	3430-3885	3870-4240	3790-4605	3914-4535
Wheelbases, Ins.	118	118	118	118	118	119	119	122	122, 125	126, 128
8 Cyl. Engines, BHP	110	112	125	125	161	188, 198	210-235	255-290	235-360	210-345

The Muntz Jet was one of those interesting "shoestring" cars that sprang up in the expansive Fifties, when many believed that a dream and a little money were all it took to make it big in the auto business. The dreamer here was Earl "Madman" Muntz, that irrepressible radio/TV manufacturer whose wild-and-woolly advertising also made him Southern California's largest—and most flamboyant—used-car dealer by the early Fifties. Typical of his sales pitches: "I wanna give 'em away, but Mrs. Muntz won't let me. She's *ca-RAAA-zy!*"

Muntz's car actually originated with Frank Kurtis, the famed designer of winning race cars—especially dirt-track midgets—who turned his enormous talents to a street sports car in 1948. His resulting Kurtis Sport was a slab-sided two-seat convertible that was unusual for its day in having a unit body/chassis with just 10 outer panels, all aluminum except for a fiberglass hood and rear deck. Appearance was bulbous but pleasing on a tight 100-inch wheelbase, and it served safety with a full-perimeter rub rail and a large bumper/grille on rubber shock absorbers—a forecast of the "safety" bumpers we'd love to hate in the Seventies. The cockpit was handsomely furnished with full instrumentation ahead of a big steering wheel on an axially adjustable column. Side windows were clumsy, clip-in Plexiglas affairs, but a removable rigid top was provided along with the expected soft top.

Like interior hardware, the Kurtis's suspension and running gear were mainly proprietary components, though Frank tuned spring and damper rates for optimum handling and roadholding. The powerteam was anything the buyer wanted, though 239-cubic-inch Ford flathead V-8s with Edelbrock manifolds were fitted to most examples. The Sport was also offered as a kit at $1495-$3495, depending on completeness.

Light weight gave the Sport good go despite the flathead's meager 100 horsepower, and reviewers loved the car's nimbleness and stability. But Frank's Kurtis-Kraft was a small company building cars mostly by hand, so after seeing just 36 Sports out the door through 1950, Frank sold his Glendale, California, operation to the "Madman" for $200,000.

Earl set about making the Sport more saleable, retaining its basic styling but adding 13 inches to wheelbase, a back seat, and more conveniences. This meant extra weight, so Cadillac's new 160-horsepower, 331-cid overhead-valve

1954 Muntz Jet convertible coupe

V-8 was substituted for the Ford flathead.

Working out of the former Kurtis plant, Muntz built 28 Jets before moving the operation to his hometown of Evanston, Illinois, just north of Chicago, and making more substantial design changes. The aluminum body gave way to a steel shell striding a new 116-inch wheelbase. Curiously, the modern Cadillac engine was ditched for Lincoln's old 336.7-cid flathead V-8 modified to produce 154 bhp. GM Hydra-Matic transmission was made standard, though Borg-Warner overdrive was available.

"We tooled that car for $75,000," Muntz later recalled. But labor costs were a monumental $2000 per car because body panels had to be carefully fitted, then leaded-in. Meticulous detailing was required elsewhere. "Today the labor in that s.o.b. would run 20 grand!" he said in 1985. The actual costs were bad enough. "I lost $400,000 on that project before we closed it down in 1954"—about $1000 per car. "They cost $6500 apiece to build, and at that price they wouldn't sell. At $5500 I couldn't make enough of 'em, but I couldn't afford to keep it up."

The Evanston cars weighed 400 pounds more than the Glendale Jets—about 3780 pounds—but were more durable. Both versions were decently quick. Lincoln-powered Jets could do 0-60 in a tick over 12 seconds and see near 108 mph. A good thing, then, that seatbelts and dash padding were standard, years before Ford tried selling safety. The Madman also pointed to his car's fully boxed perimeter frame. "The goddamn thing was built like a tank, [though] had we continued, I think we'd have lightened it. [But] in a demolition derby it'd ruin everything!" Near the end of the car's run, Muntz switched to fiberglass fenders and Lincoln's 160-bhp ohv V-8.

Even Earl didn't seem to know for sure, but it's estimated that 490 Jets were built; of these, at least 49 survive today. Undaunted by his relative failure in the car business, Muntz returned to making—and hawking—radios and TVs, ever optimistic, ever successful, ever "ca-RAAA-zy." Later he'd pioneer the stereo cartridge tape and big-screen television. "My work is my hobby, my love, my life," he once said. Sadly, his colorful life came to an end in late 1987, and we're all a little poorer for it.

MUNTZ AT A GLANCE			
Model Year	1950*	1951-52*	1953-54*
Price Range, $	4000	4450	5500
Weight Range, Lbs.	3300	3700	3560
Wheelbases, Ins.	113	116	116
8 Cyl. Engines, BHP	160	154	160

*production years; Muntz did not observe formal model years.

Nash died in 1957, the same year as Hudson. That was no coincidence. Out of desperation, the two old-line independents had linked up to form American Motors in 1954. But they entered this marriage for somewhat different reasons. Hudson was destitute, having stuck too long with its big "Step-Down" models, and further drained of cash by a slow-selling compact. Nash, on the other hand, had a very good-selling compact, but it, too, couldn't seem to build standard cars that sold well enough to prevent the inevitable.

Nevertheless, Nash innovated more than most automakers in the Fifties. Credit George Mason, one of the few truly visionary executives to lead an independent in the postwar period. Mason became Nash-Kelvinator chairman in 1948, just in time to introduce the radical 1949 Airflyte. Continued through '51, it was not only the most radical Nash ever, but one of the most advanced cars of its day.

The Airflyte was cooked up during World War II by veteran Nash engineer Nils Erik Wahlberg and Ted Ulrich, who'd helped design the unitized '41 Nash while at Budd Body Company and was hired by Wahlberg on the strength of that car's success. The way-out "bathtub" styling was the work of Holden "Bob" Koto, who with partner Ted Pietsch in 1943 showed Wahlberg a small scale model very much like the eventual production design. Wahlberg must have liked it, for he'd experimented with streamlined cars in wind-tunnel tests. The Airflyte was thus very "slick" aerodynamically, with only 113 pounds of drag at 60 mph versus up to 171 pounds for the similar-looking '49 Packard.

Maintaining Nash's two-series postwar lineup, the '49 Airflyte came in "600" models, again on a 112-inch wheelbase, and as Ambassadors on their usual 121-inch span (the extra length was entirely ahead of the firewall). Each series listed two- and four-door sedans and "Brougham" club coupes, all bulbous fastbacks. Engines were also unchanged from 1946-48: a 172.6 cubic-inch L-head six with 82 horsepower for "600s" (bore and stroke: 3.13 × 3.75 inches), a 234.8-cid overhead-valve version (3.38 × 4.38) with 112 bhp for Ambassadors. The Nash six, a hardy seven-main-bearing unit respected since its 1928 debut, would have one of Detroit's longest production runs, continuing all the way through 1956.

Airflytes were chockablock with novelties: one-piece curved windshield, "Uniscope" gauge cluster (in a pod atop the steering column), dual inward-facing rear seats on Broughams (separated by a "card table" armrest) and, after '49, optional seatbelts and reclining right-front seat (dealers sold pneumatic mattresses as accessories). Those seats plus Nash-Kelvinator's famed "Weather-Eye" heating/ventilation system made Airflytes the most habitable long-distance cars in America.

With the postwar seller's market still in full swing, the Airflyte sold very well—better than any big Nashes before. Some 142,600 were built for '49, rocketing Nash into the industry's top 10 for the first time. The 1950 total was near 172,000—an all-time company record, though that included some 58,000 of the new compact Ramblers.

1950 Nash Ambassador Super four-door sedan

1950 Nash Ambassador Super four-door sedan

Optional Hydra-Matic Drive (purchased from GM) arrived for 1950, when "600" was renamed Statesman and given a stroked 184-cid engine (3.13 × 4.00) making three extra horsepower. Rear windows were enlarged to improve visibility, though that remained pretty bad. Prices remained competitive: under $2000 for Statesmans, $2060-$2200 for Ambassadors. For 1951 came extended and raised rear fenders that softened the "beetleback" look, plus new grilles and, for Ambassadors, three more horsepower. As in 1950, trim levels comprised base Deluxe, mid-range Super, and top-shelf Custom, an arrangement Nash would keep for most of the rest of its days. Prices again changed little, but the public had quickly tired of "bathtub" styling, and Airflyte production eased to about 103,600.

The new 100-inch-wheelbase 1950 Rambler was the very antithesis of the huge Airflyte. Though several Detroit makers had attempted smaller cars before World War II, Rambler was the first to sell in significant volume. Interestingly, Ford and Chevrolet had considered compacts—and quickly discarded them—right after the war, but their concepts were quite different from Nash's. As George Romney, then Mason's top assistant, once said: "It's one thing for a small company—a marginal firm—to pioneer a new concept like that and really push it. But it's another thing for people who already have a big slice to begin pushing something that undercuts their basic market." Still, the Rambler's early sales success did not go unnoticed at the Big Three, and they would follow Nash's lead, though they took 10 years to do it.

Small cars ever fascinated George Mason, who knew

1951 Nash Statesman Super four-door sedan

1951 Nash Rambler Custom Country Club hardtop coupe

1952 Nash Ambassador Super four-door sedan

1953 Nash-Healey roadster by Pinin Farina

1954 Nash Metropolitan convertible coupe

that the independents couldn't hope to survive in the postwar market without offering cars the Big Three didn't. Together with chief engineer Meade Moore, Mason hammered away until the Rambler (and later, the Metropolitan) was a reality. It arrived just as the sell-anything era was ending, and it would keep Nash's head above water until it merged with Hudson. After 1957, AMC would sell nothing but Ramblers.

The 1950 Rambler saw little change through 1952. Only two models were offered initially: Custom two-door wagon and the interesting Custom Landau convertible with fixed side-window frames. A pretty hardtop coupe called Country Club was added for '51, but most sales came from the practical, attractive wagons (called Suburban after '51). In those early days of all-steel models, Rambler accounted for 22 percent of total U.S. wagon sales. All these Ramblers carried Nash's smaller 172.6-cid six with 82 bhp—good for 25-30 mpg, said the company. The '52s maintained the 1950-51 sales pace, recording just over 53,000.

Quotable road-tester Tom McCahill of *Mechanix Illustrated* magazine once wrote that Mason and Nash were "busier than a mouse in a barrel of hungry cats." Perhaps as proof, Mason also busied himself with a sports car in these years. Called Nash-Healey, it started with a chance meeting aboard the *Queen Elizabeth* between Mason and famed British sports-car builder Donald Healey, then looking to buy American engines. The result of their chat debuted in 1951 as a low, slab-sided two-seat roadster with 102-inch wheelbase, British-crafted aluminum body, and an Ambassador six tuned for 125 bhp. Healey assembled it at his small works in Warwick, England.

The Nash-Healey perfectly expressed Mason's "be different or die" attitude, but it cost a bunch—over $4000 at first—and thus didn't sell well: 104 of the '51s, 150 for '52, 162 of the '53s, and just 90 for '54 (including a few leftovers reserialed as '55 models). Even so, the N-H became better as it went along. Handsome steel bodywork shaped by Italy's Pinin Farina arrived for 1952. The next year brought a six-inch longer wheelbase for a companion coupe called Le Mans (honoring high N-H finishes at the French 24-hour race in 1951-52). Nash also offered a 140-bhp dual-carburetor option, but canceled the roadster after '53. The high cost of transatlantic shipping pushed the price over $6000 by the end, but every Nash-Healey was a genuine dual-purpose sports car: quick and nimble on the road, strong enough for the track.

Because Mason so liked Farina's Nash-Healey restyle, he asked the designer to shape a new big Nash for 1952. Farina submitted two proposals, but the end product was mostly the doing of Nash's own Edmund A. Anderson; its only surviving Farina elements were a simple square grille and three-element wrapped rear window. Still, the '52 Statesmans and Ambassadors wore "PF" badges just like post-'51 N-Hs, and were squarishly good-looking notchbacks. Nash called them "Golden Airflytes," honoring its 50th birthday that year. Alas, integral front fender skirts, as on previous Airflytes, made for huge turning circles and difficult tire-changing.

Nash's '52 offerings comprised Super and Custom two- and four-door sedans plus a new Custom Country Club hardtop in each line. Statesmans, however, now rode a 114.3-inch-wheelbase and carried a stroked 195.6-cid six (3.13 × 4.25) with 88 bhp. Prices moved up: $2150-$2400 for Statesmans, $2520-$2830 for Ambassadors.

The '53s were identified only by small chrome spacers on their cowl airscoops (part of the "Weather-Eye" system). Nash still billed itself as "America's travel car" with things like a drawer-type glovebox and a full-width parcel net above the windshield, but those were just masks for tepid performance. To perk things up for '53, Nash booted the Statesman to 100 bhp and offered Ambassadors with dual carbs and high-compression aluminum head in a 140-bhp "Le Mans" option, as on the N-H.

An attractive new "floating" grille arrived for '54, when Custom two-door sedans were eliminated and the Statesman got its own dual-carb option: a 110-bhp setup dubbed "Dual Powerflyte." That surely raised eyebrows at Chrysler (which had its new PowerFlite automatic transmission that year), but Nash probably got away with it because sales had been steadily dropping: down to 154,000 for '52, then 121,000 and finally 91,000 for '54. More ominously, the low-profit Ramblers—nicely updated for '53 via a clean single-bar grille—accounted for a growing portion of this withering pie.

And Nash had something even smaller for '54: a tiny two-seater on an 85-inch-wheelbase. Called Metropolitan, it began with an early postwar prototype styled by independent designer Bill Flajole, which was displayed to select audiences during 1950 as the NXI (for "Nash Xperimental International"). Response was favorable, but Mason didn't arrange for production until late 1953. Bodies were contracted to the well-known Fisher & Ludlow works in Birmingham, England, and final assembly to Austin in Longbridge. Austin also donated its A40 model's four-cylinder engine, an elderly long-stroke bit of ironmongery that extracted 42 bhp from 73.8 cid.

The Metropolitan arrived in hardtop and convertible models priced around $1450. Weight was just over 1800 pounds, so mileage was good: up to 40 mpg. At first, sales were pretty good, too, with Austin shipping 13,905 through late '54. But demand fell to just under 6100 the next year, prompting some changes for '56.

Meanwhile, the big "Farina" Nashes were facelifted for 1955, acquiring raised front wheel arches at last, plus wrapped windshield and a smart new oval grille encircling the headlights. Cooperation between the new AMC and Studebaker-Packard (another 1954 merger) gave Nash its first eight-cylinder cars since 1942: Ambassadors with that year's new Packard-built V-8 of 320 cid (3.81 × 3.50) and 208 bhp. The Ambassador Eight was much quicker than the Six, though it cost $300 more. Two-door sedans departed, but other models stayed. As in '54, Statesmans had 100 standard bhp, Ambassador Sixes 130, and both again offered power-packs adding 10 bhp.

Rambler also got exposed front wheels for '55, plus an eggcrate grille and its first four-doors: sedans and Cross

1954 Nash Ambassador Custom four-door sedan

1955 Nash Statesman Custom Country Club hardtop coupe

1956 Nash Ambassador Super four-door sedan

Country wagons on a new 108-inch wheelbase, again with unitized body/chassis. Two-doors retained the original 100-inch chassis. All body styles offered a choice of Deluxe, Super, and Custom trim. Rambler had adopted larger sixes in '53: the old 184 and 195 engines with 85 and 90 bhp, respectively. The smaller unit disappeared for '55, but the larger version now came in 90- and 100-bhp tune.

With Ramblers still popular and Nash newly married to moribund Hudson, '55 Ramblers were sold through both dealer networks—with appropriate badges, of course. The same would apply to 1955-56 Metropolitans. But this tended to obscure the fact that the big Nashes were failing as much as the big Hudsons. In a model year when most every Detroit car sold well, Statesman/Ambassador managed but 40,056 units—not even half the '54 tally.

Accordingly, Rambler got all the emphasis for '56 under new AMC president Romney (who took over on Mason's untimely death in 1954). A full outer-body reskin brought a wrapped windshield, squarish eggcrate grille with inboard headlights, blocky body contours, and colorful

1957 Nash Ambassador Custom four-door sedan

1957 Nash Ambassador Custom Country Club hardtop coupe

early Mets only did about 70 mph tops, the 1500 could approach 80, though it was still no sports car. Styling was updated by a mesh grille with prominent new "M" medallion, a hood shorn of dummy airscoop, and zigzag side moldings that delineated loud two-tone paint schemes (one stylist likened the result to Neapolitan ice cream). Though prices were hiked to $1500-$1600, the Met would continue to find favor through decade's end. Sales averaged 14,000 a year for 1957-58, then jumped to 22,300 for '59. But the bubble quickly burst, and the Met would depart in 1962. Since then, these cute little cars have become "cult collectibles." Who would have thought it?

Far less unthinkable in 1956 was the end of the big Nash. That year's lineup was cut to Statesman and Ambassador Six Super Sedans, plus V-8 Ambassador Super and Custom sedans and Custom Country Club. The V-8s retained Packard power through April, then became Ambassador Specials by switching to AMC's own new 327 V-8 (4.00 × 3.25) with 190 bhp. Ed Anderson devised big "lollipop" taillights, extra chrome for the sides and front end, and splashy duotone and tri-tone paint schemes, but they were little help. Model-year production amounted to just 22,709.

Nash got one more chance, but its 1957 was anticlimactic. Side trim was shuffled, and headlamps not only moved back to the fenders but multiplied to stack in pairs astride a busy oval grille. Models were limited to Super and Custom Ambassador sedans and Country Clubs, with Customs often heroically overcolored. All carried more potent 327 V-8, developing 255 bhp via four-barrel carb, dual exhausts, and 9:1 compression.

But the bell had been tolling for some time, so after 1957 production of just 3561 big cars, Nash was laid to rest alongside Hudson. It was purely a survival move. AMC was still digging out from the debts incurred from the Nash-Hudson merger, and the Rambler name had become a far more saleable commodity, to say nothing of the cars. At least the Ambassador didn't die, returning as a 1958 line of stretched Ramblers once planned for Nash and Hudson. The once-proud Nash name would hang on all the way through 1974.

exteriors with optional two-tone and even three-tone paint jobs. What's more, all Ramblers were on the 108-inch wheelbase and had four doors. Some lacked B-posts, though, as airy hardtop sedans and Detroit's first hardtop *wagons* were added. Horsepower was boosted to 120 across the board. Prices were higher, but still reasonable: $1830-$2330. These Ramblers also wore Nash and Hudson badges for sale through the separate dealer nets. About 10,000 were built for the model year, after which Rambler became a separate make. (See "Rambler" for 1957-59 information.)

Also new for '56 was an improved Metropolitan, the 1500. That referred to the metric displacement of an upsized 90.9-cid Austin four (2.88 × 3.50), which churned out 52 bhp, 24 percent more than the old "1200." Where

NASH AT A GLANCE										
Model Year	**1950**	**1951**	**1952**	**1953**	**1954**	**1955**	**1956**	**1957**	**1958**	**1959**
Price Range, $	1633-2223	1841-4063	2003-5868	2003-5899	1550-4721	1457-5128	2146-3072	2820-3100		
Weight Range, Lbs.	2430-3390	2420-3445	2420-3550	2550-3550-	1803-3575	1803-3839	3199-3854	3639-3722		
Wheelbases, Ins.	100-121	100-121	100-121.25	100-121.25	100-121.25	100-121.25	114, 121.25	121.25		
4 Cyl. Engines, BHP					42	42	42, 52	52		
6 Cyl. Engines, BHP	82-115	82-125	82-125	85-140	85-140	90-140	130, 135			
8 Cyl. Engines, BHP						208	190, 220	255		

No General Motors make was better prepared for the high-flying Fifties than Oldsmobile. Already established as GM's "innovator," Olds had introduced self-shift Hydra-Matic Drive back in 1940 and Harley Earl's first postwar styling in the 1948 "Futuramic 98." For 1949, Olds applied Futuramic design to all its models, and shared honors with Cadillac and Buick in pioneering the hardtop-convertible with its 98 Holiday, an idea that would see overwhelming acceptance in the Fifties.

But Oldsmobile's most historic achievement of this period was undoubtedly the modern high-compression overhead-valve V-8, another '49 development (again shared with Cadillac). Aptly called "Rocket," it made Oldsmobile a hot performer on both stock-car tracks and new-car sales charts. Indeed, Olds has never soared higher than it did in this decade, rocketing to fourth in industry production for 1955 and '58.

The Rocket V-8 was designed chiefly by Gilbert Burrell, and independently of Cadillac's new '49 engine. GM management had encouraged the divisions to outdo each other, and Cadillac actually raised displacement to maintain a "proper distance" from Oldsmobile's new engine. The Rocket arrived at 303.7 cubic inches; Cadillac started at 309, then went to 331 cid.

A five-main-bearing unit with oversquare dimensions (bore and stroke: 3.75×3.44 inches), the Rocket was initially rated at 135 horsepower. Originally, it was destined only for the senior C-body 98s, which weighed close to two tons. But at the last minute, Olds general manager Sherrod Skinner decided to pocket the Rocket in the lighter 119.5-inch B-body Series 76, ousting an old 257.1-cid "stroker" six (3.53×4.38) with but 105 bhp. The result was 1949's new Futuramic 88 with a power-to-weight ratio of about 22.5 pounds/bhp—quite good for the era. Torque was also impressive at 240 pounds-feet. Compression was a mild 7.25:1 at first, but could go as high as 12:1. Engineers had anticipated postwar fuels with ultra-high octane, though the levels never were quite high enough to require such ratios.

With so much new, Olds had a rollicking 1949, scoring production of 288,000-plus. The 1950 total was higher still at near 408,000, helped by new 76 and 88 Holiday hardtops.

That year's junior Oldsmobiles received a mild update of their aircraft-inspired '49 styling, but the big 98s were lower and more massive-looking, this despite a three-inch shorter 122-inch wheelbase, thanks to a new GM C-body complete with one-piece windshield. They came as standard- and DeLuxe-trim two- and four-door notchback sedans, the same with fastback styling, the Holidays, plus Deluxe convertible. The 76 and 88 deleted four-door fastbacks for four-door wagons, which were all-steel now—Lansing's first—though they looked like the part-wood models they'd displaced in mid-1949.

To no one's surprise, the fleet "Rocket 88s" promptly began rewriting the stock-car racing record book, claiming three consecutive NASCAR championships (1949-51). Six of the nine NASCAR Grand Nationals in 1949 fell to Olds, with "Red" Byron the national driving champ. In

1950 Oldsmobile Futuramic 88 convertible coupe

1950 Oldsmobile Futuramic 98 DeLuxe Club Sedan two-door

1951 Oldsmobile Super 88 two-door sedan

1951 Oldsmobile 98 DeLuxe Holiday hardtop coupe

1952 Oldsmobile Super 88 four-door sedan

1950 an 88 broke the class speed record at Daytona with a two-way average of 100.28 mph. That same year, an 88 won the first Mexican Road Race, besting such formidable competitors as Alfa Romeo, Cadillac, and Lincoln. On the stock-car ovals Olds was 10 for 19 in 1950 and 20 for 41 in '51. Though displaced by the Hudson Hornet in 1952-54, the 88s continued to show their mettle. Paul Frere, for example, drove one to victory in a 1952 stock-car event at Spa in Belgium, and a 1950 model nicknamed "Roarin' Relic" was still winning the occasional modified race as late as 1959.

Such goings-on naturally kept sales going once the post-war boom market went bust in 1950. Olds tapered off to 213,500 for '52 but was back to 354,000 by 1954, when it placed fifth in the production race. Olds then passed Plymouth to claim fourth for '55. Interestingly, the division managed these triumphs with only three basic series and no station wagons for 1951-56.

The big event of 1951 was the new Super 88 with a 120-inch wheelbase and styling much like that of the facelifted 98. Canceling the six-cylinder 76 line—who needed it with the Rocket around?—left 88 the base series with just two- and four-door sedans. The 98 was trimmed to a sedan, convertible, and Holiday hardtop, the last still available in standard and DeLuxe versions. The Futuramic label was abandoned as styling became more "important," though the grille was formed by simple bars and side decoration was minimal. This basic appearance continued for '52, when the 88 became a detrimmed Super with a retuned 145-bhp Rocket; other models moved up to 160 bhp.

Along with the Cadillac Eldorado and Buick Skylark, 1953 brought a limited-production Olds convertible, the Fiesta, a $5717 mid-year addition to the 98 line. Custom leather interior, wraparound "Panoramic" windshield, and a special 170-bhp V-8 distinguished it from the normal 98 ragtop. Hydra-Matic, power brakes and steering, and hydraulic servos for windows and seats were all standard. So were distinctive spinner wheel covers soon copied by most every accessory house in the business, appearing on hot rods and custom cars from coast to coast. Only 458 Fiestas were built and the model was dropped after '53, but it did serve as a styling preview of the next-generation Olds.

That styling arrived on 1954's new B- and C-bodies bearing squared-up below-the-belt sheetmetal, fully wrapped windshields, wrapped back windows, and distinctive L-shape bodyside moldings that delineated contrast color areas on some two-toned models. This was arguably Oldsmobile's most attractive car of the Fifties. Happily, its basic look would persist through 1956.

So would body styles: 88 and Super 88 two- and four-door sedans and Holiday hardtop; Super 88 convertible;

1954 Oldsmobile 98 Fiesta convertible coupe

1954 Oldsmobile Ninety-Eight DeLuxe Holiday hardtop coupe

1954 Oldsmobile Super 88 Holiday hardtop coupe

1955 Oldsmobile Super 88 DeLuxe Holiday hardtop coupe

1955 Oldsmobile Ninety-Eight DeLuxe Holiday hardtop sedan

1956 Oldsmobile Ninety-Eight Starfire convertible coupe

98 Holiday, Deluxe Holiday, Deluxe sedan, and Starfire convertible. Holiday four-door hardtops arrived at mid-1955, half a year ahead of every other make's save Buick's (which bowed along with Oldsmobile's). Wheelbases shifted for '54 to 122 inches for 88/Super 88 and 126 for 98, and would stay there through 1957. Also for '54, the Rocket was bored out to 324 cid (3.88 × 3.44) to deliver 170 bhp in 88s, 185 in Super 88s and 98s. But with Detroit's "horsepower race" escalating, the figures were duly bumped to 185/202 for '55, then to 230/240 bhp.

Olds set another record by building over 50 percent more cars for '55 than '54—some 553,000—and claimed fourth in the industry. A substantial facelift gave the '55s a bold oval grille and jazzier two-toning. The '56s gained a large, gaping "mouth" front like that of the 1953 Starfire show car. Despite a general industry retreat, the division did quite well to turn out some 485,000 of its '56s, though Plymouth's return to fourth pushed Olds down a spot on the production chart.

Another new B- and C-body arrived for 1957 with sleeker styling and the first Olds wagons since 1950. Called Fiesta, the new haulers comprised a pillared 88 four-door and pillarless 88 and Super 88 models, the latter reflecting the public's passion for hardtop styling. Both 88 series were subtitled Golden Rocket (after a 1956 show car) in honor of Oldsmobile's 50th birthday; 98s gained Starfire as a first name. The Rocket was again enlarged, this time both ways to 371.1 cid (4.00 × 3.69), good for 277 bhp. But that was just for starters. To bolster its "hot car" image—and maybe stock-car racing fortunes—Olds offered a three-by-two-barrel carburetor option coded "J-2" that lifted bhp to 300. Installed in one of the lighter 88s—as it often was for "stockers"—the J-2 could deliver 0-60 mph in less than eight seconds.

The '57 Olds was rather clean for a GM car that year. The wide-mouth grille was mildly reshaped; windshield pillars were more rakishly angled; a broad, stainless-steel sweepspear dropped down from the middle of the belt, then shot straight back to the tail, thus defining a two-toning area; and there were finless rear fenders ending in peaked, roughly circular taillamps. But GM styling was looking passe next to Virgil Exner's Forward Look at Chrysler; Harley Earl's reign as America's automotive styling arbiter was coming to a close. Still, Olds built nearly 385,000 cars and again finished fifth.

While most makes faltered badly in recession 1958, Olds reclaimed fourth, though on reduced volume near the 315,000 mark. Model offerings stood pat except that two-door sedans were now limited to the base series, renamed Dynamic 88. Wheelbases stretched a nominal half-inch on all models. Styling, most observers concluded, was atrocious. Ford designer Alex Tremulis satirized Oldsmobile's four horizontal rear-fender chrome strips by drawing in a clef and a few notes of music on a photograph. Yet for all the overchromed dazzle, Olds sold pretty well—aided, no doubt, by more power choices: 265 bhp for 88s (a sop to buyers suddenly concerned with fuel economy), 305 bhp on Supers, and a 312-bhp J-2 setup for 98s (optional elsewhere).

1956 Oldsmobile Super 88 convertible coupe

1958 Oldsmobile Golden Rocket Super 88 Fiesta hardtop station wagon

1957 Oldsmobile Golden Rocket Super 88 Holiday hardtop coupe

1958 Oldsmobile Dynamic 88 Holiday hardtop coupe

1958 Oldsmobile Super 88 Holiday hardtop coupe

1959 Oldsmobile Super 88 SceniCoupe hardtop

1959 Oldsmobile Ninety-Eight Holiday hardtop sedan

had repercussions. Chevy and Pontiac, for example, had to drop their all-new '58 platforms after only a year; Olds, Buicks, and Cadillac after two years. Still, this move held production costs down, thus enabling the company to put that much more time and money into a squadron of new compacts.

As ever, divisional styling strived for distinct looks, though the '59 Olds ended up more like Pontiac than Lansing might have liked. With a new emphasis on "Wide-Track" handling, Pontiac outpaced Olds in production, something it hadn't done since 1953.

But Lansing's '59s were hardly slim, swelling nine inches wider on a new "Guard-Beam" chassis. They were also 10 inches longer. Naturally they shared basic elements of the new corporate styling: vastly enlarged "Vista-Panoramic" windshields, curving non-dogleg A-posts, big rear windows (fully wrapped on new Holiday Sport-Sedan hardtops), thin-section coupe rooflines, narrow pillars, and fuller lower body sheetmetal. To this Olds added a simple dumbbell-shaped grille with four widely spaced headlights and straight-topped rear fenders with teeny fins above oval taillights. Division ad types called all this "The Linear Look."

No matter: The '59s were a vast improvement on the sparkling '58s, though there were still gadgets aplenty, including "New-Matic Ride," Lansing's year-old version of air suspension that was costly, unpopular, and about to disappear. At least power was still plentiful, if down a bit: Dynamics and Supers retained 371 V-8s, with 270 and 300 respective bhp. New for 98s was a bored-out 394 (4.13 × 3.69) making 315 bhp with slightly reduced 9.75:1 compression and four-barrel carb. Less obvious were the many internal changes made to this year's Rocket, as well as the "Jet-Away" Hydra-Matic long ordered by most Olds buyers. For 1959, said buyers could choose from a convertible, two- and four-door Holidays, and a pillared Celebrity sedan in each line, plus Dynamic 88 two-door sedan and two-seat Dynamic and Super Fiesta wagons.

On balance, 1959 was a good Olds year, the division scoring another fifth-place finish on slightly improved volume of nearly 383,000 units. Though its cars had come a long way from the first 88s, Olds still retained something of a performance image, which it would shine anew to great success in the Sixties.

The '59s might have looked even worse, but GM responded to Chrysler's '57 models with a crash effort that produced much cleaner styling than first planned—and a significant divisional body realignment. Chevy and Pontiac would now share the corporate A-body, the junior Buicks, and Oldsmobiles a new B-body, and senior models a slightly different C-body with Cadillac. Olds and Buick wheelbases were set at 123 and 126 inches. Pontiac's was slightly shorter, Chevy's shorter still. This program

OLDSMOBILE AT A GLANCE										
Model Year	1950	1951	1952	1953	1954	1955	1956	1957	1958	1959
Price Range, $	1719-2772	2049-3025	2262-3229	2262-5715	2272-3249	2297-3276	2422-3740	2733-4217	2772-4300	2837-4366
Weight Range, Lbs.	3260-4150	3507-4107	3565-4111	3603-4453	3699-4193	3688-4159	3691-4325	3963-4572	3972-4391	4040-4485
Wheelbases, Ins.	119.5, 122	119.5-122	120, 124	120, 124	122, 126	122, 126	122, 126	122, 126	122.5, 126.5	123, 126
6 Cyl. Engines, BHP	105									
8 Cyl. Engines, BHP	135	135	145, 160	150-170	170, 185	185, 202	230, 240	277-300	265-312	270-315

Packard, that patrician stalwart of American automobiles, purchased ailing Studebaker in 1954. The result, as one employee said later, was like was "two drunks trying to help each other across the road." Packard never made it to the other side, expiring in 1958 after a half-hearted run of Studebaker-based models. Though was Packard clearly sacrificed to save Studebaker, there were plenty of other problems that set the stage for Packard's ultimate demise.

They started with the 1950 models, last of the so-called "pregnant elephants" introduced for 1948. Heavy in appearance as well as fact, they were a literal outgrowth of the advanced, prewar Clipper line of envelope-bodied sedans and coupes. Designed by the redoubtable Howard A. "Dutch" Darrin, ably assisted by Packard Styling under Werner Gubitz, the good-looking Clipper proved immediately popular. Trouble was, it arrived less than a year before Pearl Harbor, and World War II stopped production almost before it began.

When peace returned in 1945, Packard followed most other Detroit makers in reprising 1941-42 models. But other companies wrung a good deal more production from their prewar tooling, and were able to field new all-postwar designs in 1948-49—most ahead of the Clipper in style. Though Packard emerged from the war in good financial shape (from building marine and Rolls-Royce Merlin aero engines), it couldn't afford to junk the Clipper dies because they hadn't been amortized by sufficient production.

Accordingly, Packard stylists loaded extra sheetmetal onto the Clipper, eliminating the separate fenders and narrow, tapered hood/grille. The result was a 1948 line of ungainly Eights and Super Eights on 120-inch wheelbases and Custom Eights on a standard 127-inch platform. Auto writer Tom McCahill said they looked ready to be driven "by a dowager in a Queen Mary hat."

Packard made another postwar mistake by continuing to emphasize medium-priced cars pitched $500 or so below the cheapest Cadillacs and Lincolns. This, of course, stemmed from the firm's Depression-era strategy with the One-Twenty and One-Ten models, which not only saved Packard but transformed it from a low-volume builder of high-quality cars to mass-production automaker. Yet Packard had always been synonymous with prestige, and most historians agree that its luxury image was fatally squandered by the continued postwar reliance on cheaper models. Both Cadillac and Lincoln returned to pure luxury products much sooner than Packard did, and thus sold volumes more high-priced cars, with obvious benefits to profit margins. Packard thus found itself with just three percent of the luxury market by 1952.

None of this suggests that the "elephants" weren't good automobiles. Packard engineering always rated high, and the cars were beautifully engineered, with surprisingly roadable suspensions and big, smooth, low-revving straight eights. From mid-1949, Packard could also boast Ultramatic, its first fully automatic transmission—and the only one developed by an independent without outside help. Ultramatic combined a torque converter with multi-

1950 Packard Custom Eight four-door sedan

1951 Packard 250 convertible coupe

1951 Packard 250 Mayfair hardtop coupe

ple-disc and direct-drive clutches, plus forward/reverse bands. The car started from rest using the torque converter, then shifted into direct mechanical drive at about 15 miles an hour. But though smoother than GM's Hydra-Matic, it provided only leisurely acceleration, and frequent use of Low range for faster starts caused premature wear.

Still, while the postwar seller's market lasted, it didn't matter whether a Packard sold for $2500 or $4500. Like most everyone else in these years, Packard could sell every car it built. And indeed, production totaled some 92,000 for '48 and about 116,000 for '49, two of Packard's best years ever. But the seller's market ended in 1950, and Packard production showed it, plunging to just under 42,400.

Packard finally managed a total redesign for 1951

adopting John Reinhart's squarish but praiseworthy "high-pockets" notchback shape, a complete—and welcome—break from the "elephants." A 122-inch wheelbase supported a new "200" series of standard and DeLuxe two- and four-door sedans, plus a spiffy "250" convertible and Mayfair hardtop coupe. A 127-inch chassis rode beneath "300" and Patrician 400 sedans. The 200s, though powered by the same 288-cubic-inch straight eight (bore and stroke: 3.50 × 3.75) as the previous Packard Eight, weren't Packards in the traditional sense. The line even included a $2302 business coupe, $529 less than the cheapest '51 Cadillac. But with the seller's market ended, the 200s couldn't sell well against established price rivals.

The "real" Packards of 1951 were the 250s, which did sell pretty well, and the regal 300 and Patrician. At just under $3800, the Patrician effectively replaced the previous broad Custom Eight line that carried a mammoth 160-bhp 356-cid straight eight weighing almost 1000 pounds. But though very smooth and utterly reliable, the 356 cost too much to build in light of expected sales, so Packard's biggest '51 engine was a destroked 327 version (3.50 × 4.25), previously the middle powerplant, also with nine main bearings and nearly as much horsepower: 155 for Patricians and Ultramatic 250/300s, 150 otherwise.

Overall, Packard's new '51 package fared quite well—probably because it *was* new in a year when little else was. Model-year production ended at 95,672—more than twice the dismal 1950 total. (Packard also built 401 "300" chassis that year for what remained of its once-thriving custom-body business.)

But 1952 production was down substantially, sliding to 62,921 (plus 320 chassis). Changes were few. The 200 business coupe was dropped, power brakes arrived as a first-time option, and there were colorful new interior treatments of high-quality fabric and leather done up by fashion designer Dorothy Draper. Exterior appearance was virtually untouched, however. The most obvious change was a different wing position for the traditional Packard pelican hood ornament.

A far more significant change occurred in the executive suite during 1952. In May, Packard's aging president Hugh Ferry stepped down in favor of James J. Nance, a market-wise sales hotshot recruited from Hotpoint to turn Packard's fortunes around—or so it was hoped. Those fortunes needed a turn. By the time Nance arrived, Packard's Detroit plant was working at only 50 percent of capacity. Incredibly, several long-time executives felt that was good enough, but Nance could see then what we all see now: at that pace, Packard was doomed.

Thus did Nance aggressively seek new military business while laying out a radical new auto policy. Henceforth, he declared, the cheap 200 would be called Clipper and eventually become a separate make—which it did for 1956 (see "Clipper"). Packard meantime, would build nothing but luxury cars, including the long-wheelbase formal sedans and limousines it had lately neglected.

Lack of time, to say nothing of money, precluded a linewide makeover for '53, but Nance did see to the inclusion of an eight-passenger Executive Sedan and

"Corporation Limousine" on a massive new 149-inch chassis, priced around $7000. He even contracted with the Derham Body Company for a few formal Patricians with leather-covered tops, tiny rear windows, and $6531 price tags.

Also for the top of the '53 line, Nance pushed out the Caribbean, a glamorous convertible on the 122-inch wheelbase with colorful styling by Richard A. Teague. Inspired by the Richard Arbib-designed Packard Pan American show car of 1952 (built by Henney), the Caribbean carried a 180-bhp 327, rakish circular rear-wheel cutouts, jaunty "Continental kit" outside spare tire, and chrome wire wheels, plus most every optional amenity in the book. It cost a lofty $5210 and was deliberately limited to 750 copies—for snob appeal—but was as well-received as Cadillac's new '53 Eldorado.

Anchoring Packard's '53 line were Nance's expected Clippers: two- and four-door sedans in standard and DeLuxe guise powered by 150-bhp 288 and 160-bhp 327 engines, respectively. Included in the standard group was a snazzy new hardtop-styled pillared two-door called Sportster, attractively priced at $2805. The 250-series was defunct, but the Mayfair and standard convertible returned; the cheapest long-wheelbase '53 was a single sedan called Cavalier, replacing the 300 model.

Nance had hoped for all-new '54 Packards, but time and money were again lacking, so a lookalike interim series was offered—outwardly distinguishable by rimmed headlamps and integrated backup lights within the taillamps. The straight-eight 327, still with nine main bearings, was bored and stroked to 359 cid (3.56 × 4.50) and 212 bhp as standard for Patrician, Caribbean, and standard convertibles, commercial chassis, and a hardtop renamed Pacific. Packard had led the way to air conditioning back in 1940, and this now returned for the first time since the war. But 1954 was a terrible Packard year, with production of only 31,170 cars. Of these, some 23,000 were Clippers: comprised of Specials and DeLuxes as before, plus new Super sedans and a Super Panama hardtop coupe. As in '53, Specials used the 288 engine, but the DeLuxe's 327 was bumped up five bhp to 165; the latter also powered Supers. The Cavalier sedan used a 185-bhp version. Packard also built 335 chassis for '54.

The revolutionary new model Nance wanted for '54 was postponed to '55 partly by the so-called Studebaker-Packard merger, which was actually a Packard buyout. What Nance didn't know when he signed the papers was that Studebaker had huge productivity problems in its high-overhead South Bend plant, with a break-even point somewhere over 250,000 cars. Contrary to many accounts, Packard was still healthy at this time, but Studebaker was sinking and would drag Packard down with it.

As the all-new '55s neared production, another smoldering problem burst into flame. Back in 1940, Packard had stopped building its own bodies, contracting the work to Briggs Manufacturing Company. But Packard lost this supplier when Chrysler bought Briggs in 1954, and thus had to build its own bodies again. Inexplicably, it settled for a cramped body plant on Conner Avenue in

1952 Packard 250 Mayfair hardtop coupe

1953 Packard Clipper Club Sedan two-door

1954 Packard Pacific hardtop coupe

1955 Packard The Four Hundred hardtop coupe

1956 Packard Executive hardtop coupe

1957 Packard Clipper Town Sedan four-door

Detroit. Never big enough, this facility caused big production tie-ups and quality-control problems that hampered sales of the '55 Packards, and immediately forced cancellation of the long sedan and limo. Though Packard built some 55,250 cars for prosperous '55, it would have done better to assign body production to its old but adequate main plant on Detroit's East Grand Boulevard.

Despite these woes, the 1955 Packard was a technological marvel. Leading the list of wonders was "Torsion-Level" suspension: long torsion bars between the front and rear wheels on each side. A complex electrical system enabled the suspension to correct for load weight, and effectively interlinked all four wheels for truly extraordinary ride and handling despite two-ton bulk. And there was more: powerful new short-stroke V-8s, ousting the old-fashioned straight-eights at last. Clipper DeLuxes and Supers (now shorn of two-door sedans) used a 320-cid version (3.81 × 3.50) with 225 bhp. A bored-out 352 (4.00 × 3.50) delivered 245 bhp for new Clipper Customs (sedan and Constellation hardtop), 275 bhp in Caribbeans (via twin four-barrel carbs), and 260 bhp in Patrician and new "Four Hundred" hardtop coupe. Ultramatic was suitably modified to handle the new engines' higher torque.

With the V-8, Ultramatic, and Torsion-Level suspension, the '55s Packards had fine chassis. And despite their heft, they were impressively fast and roadable—real Packards in every sense. Styling was equally impressive. Dick Teague's clever facelift of the old '51 body produced "cathedral" taillights, peaked front fenders, an ornate grille, and a wrapped windshield. Clippers gained their own special grille and 1954-style taillights.

Some problems at the Conner plant were finally licked, but not in time for '56, when customers were scared away by Studebaker's desperate struggle as well the '55 Packards' notorious quality and service problems. Ironically, the '56s were better built.

Though Clipper was a separate make for '56, Packard still offered something like it in the short-wheelbase Executive, a sedan and hardtop announced at mid-year to bridge the price gap with Clipper, listing in the $3500-$3600 range. The longer chassis was again reserved for Patrician, Four Hundred, and two Caribbeans: the familiar convertible and a new hardtop, both with unique seat covers that could be reversed from fabric to leather. Executives wore the Clipper's pointed taillights but senior-Packard grilles, and carried the same 275-bhp 352 V-8 as the most potent '55 Packards. Other '56s used a

1958 Packard hardtop coupe

1958 Packard Hawk hardtop coupe

newly bored 374 (4.13 × 3.50) packing a mighty 310 bhp in Caribbeans and 290 bhp elsewhere. But none of this helped, and only 10,353 Packards were built for 1956, including just 263 Caribbean hardtops and 276 ragtops.

S-P had planned an all-new 1957 corporate line that included a shared bodyshell but totally different styling for Studebaker and Clipper, plus a separate, much larger platform for a group of high-luxury Packards styled in the image of Dick Teague's 1956 Predictor show car. But S-P was on the ropes, so no financial backing could be found, leading Nance to resign in August 1956. Finally, dubious salvation arrived in the form of Curtiss-Wright Corporation, which picked up S-P as a dalliance and/or tax write-off. C-W's Roy Hurley began directing S-P's affairs. One of his first decisions was to end Packard production in Detroit and substitute Studebaker-based models built in South Bend.

Thus appeared a new Packard Clipper for 1957: the infamous "Packardbaker," as many have since called it. Though a very good Studebaker, it was hardly in the same league as the last "real" Packards of 1955-56. It came in just two models: four-door Town Sedan and Country Sedan station wagon (the latter must have irked Ford), both on Studebaker's long 120-inch chassis. A supercharged Studebaker 289 V-8 (3.56 × 3.63) provided 275 bhp, as on '55 Caribbeans and '56 Executives, but Ultramatic, Torsion-Level and many other "real Packard" features were all gone. Styling, at least, played on Packard themes. Prices were higher than for comparable Studeys:

$3212/$3384. But everyone recognized this as the charade it was, and only about 5000 of the '57s (mostly sedans) were called for.

A big-Packard revival was still theoretically possible as the '58s were planned, so S-P again tried a holding action. This time there were four "Packardbakers" priced as high as $3995. Studebaker's shorter 116.5-inch platform carried a two-door hardtop and four-door wagon, the 120-inch chassis a sedan and the Packard Hawk. The last, perhaps the most famous of this series, was a more luxurious version of Studebaker's Golden Hawk.

All featured full-leather interiors and bizarre styling announced by low, "fish mouth" grilles. In defense of stylist Duncan McRae, the Hawk was really built only because of Roy Hurley, who also demanded the long, bolt-on fiberglass nose and gaudy, gold-mylar tailfins. McRae, however, gets the blame for the Hawk's outside "armrests," as well as the other three models: also garishly finned and with hastily contrived four-headlight systems intended to keep up with an industry trend. Only the Hawk was supercharged. Other '58 Packards used a normally aspirated 289 with 210 bhp. Production was uniformly low: 159 wagons, 588 Hawks, 675 hardtops, and 1200 sedans.

With that, there was no point in going on, and once-proud Packard vanished from the scene (though its name continued in the corporate title until 1962). It was a great loss, but it did give Studebaker a new lease on life, though that, too, would soon expire.

PACKARD AT A GLANCE										
Model Year	1950	1951	1952	1953	1954	1955	1956	1957	1958	1959
Price Range, $	2224-4100	2302-3662	2494-3797	2544-6531	2544-6100	2586-5932	3465-5995	3212, 3384	3212-3995	
Weight Range, Lbs.	3815-4620	3550-4115	3640-4100	3700-4720	3585-4720	3670-4755	4045-4590	3570-3650	3470-3555	
Wheelbases, Ins.	120-141	122, 127	122, 127	122-149	122-149	122, 127	122, 127	116.5, 120.5	116.5, 120.5	
8 Cyl. Engines, BHP	135-160	135-155	135-155	150-180	150-212	225-275	275-310	275	225, 275	

Oldsmobile's 1949 "Rocket" 88 sounded the gun for a "horsepower race" in Fifties Detroit that turned all manner of staid cars into stylish sizzlers. Plymouth was one of them. But more so than with Chevrolet, Pontiac, or even sister make Dodge, necessity was the mother of Plymouth's reinvention. Though unchallenged as America's number-three seller since 1932, Plymouth brand sold fewer and fewer cars after 1949, bottoming to fifth in calendar-year sales by 1954. But Chrysler Corporation's bread-and-butter brand then bounced back strongly to produce some of the decade's most exciting—and most popular—cars.

As continuations of Plymouth's new all-postwar 1949 models, its 1950-54 offerings were well-engineered, solid, and reliable, but dull and none too fast. The only engine available was a 217.8 cubic-inch L-head six (bore and stroke: 3.25 × 4.38 inches) that dated from 1934. The smallest six in Chrysler's stable, it produced 97 horsepower through 1952, then was raised to 100 bhp (probably by the stroke of an ad writer's pen). Plymouths of this period could achieve 20-23 miles per gallon, but no more than 80 mph, and then only if pressed.

The 1950 lineup was mostly a '49 reprise, with two series and two wheelbases. A 111-inch chassis supported a DeLuxe fastback two-door sedan, business coupe, and all-steel Suburban wagon; a 118.5-inch platform was used under a DeLuxe notchback coupe and four-door sedan priced in the $1500s, and a Special DeLuxe coupe, sedan, convertible, and wood-trimmed wagon covering a $1600-$2400 spread. All boasted two important new innovations for the low-price field: automatic electric choke and combined ignition/starter switch.

Though Plymouth liked to take credit for the first "modern" wagon with its Suburban, Chevy, Olds, and Pontiac also issued all-steel wagons during 1949. But Plymouth's job cost only $1840, quite a bit less than the GM models, and thus sold well. The trend picked up speed, and by 1954, the "woody" was dead.

Plymouth facelifted for 1950, adding a simpler square grille with large horizontal bar, slightly longer rear decks (to relieve the stubbiness of '49), and taillights placed low within reworked rear fenders. Even so, Plymouths and other Chrysler makes of the early Fifties were quite boxy, though roomy, comfortable, fairly compact, and easy to see out of. All this reflected the views of K.T. Keller, who'd become company president when Walter Chrysler died back in 1940. Keller was no fan of slinky "torpedo" shapes, preferring function over form, which ended up as what designers call "three-box styling"—one box atop two others. "Cars should accommodate people rather than the ideas of far-out designers," Keller once declared. Trouble was, most postwar buyers *wanted* the long, low look, never mind that it meant less headroom or ground clearance. In time, Keller's practical bent severely hampered the sales of all his company's cars.

But not in 1950, when Plymouth finished its usual third in industry volume with near 611,000 at the height of the postwar seller's market. The division repeated this performance with its 1951 models, which gained a modified

1950 Plymouth Special DeLuxe convertible coupe

1952 Plymouth Cranbrook Belvedere hardtop coupe

1952 Plymouth Cranbrook Belvedere hardtop coupe

1953 Plymouth Cranbrook convertible coupe

1953 Plymouth Cranbrook Belvedere hardtop coupe

1954 Plymouth Belvedere four-door sedan

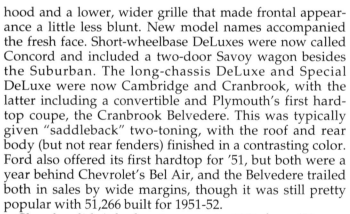

1954 Plymouth Belvedere convertible coupe

1955 Plymouth Belvedere Suburban four-door station wagon

hood and a lower, wider grille that made frontal appearance a little less blunt. New model names accompanied the fresh face. Short-wheelbase DeLuxes were now called Concord and included a two-door Savoy wagon besides the Suburban. The long-chassis DeLuxe and Special DeLuxe were now Cambridge and Cranbrook, with the latter including a convertible and Plymouth's first hardtop coupe, the Cranbrook Belvedere. This was typically given "saddleback" two-toning, with the roof and rear body (but not rear fenders) finished in a contrasting color. Ford also offered its first hardtop for '51, but both were a year behind Chevrolet's Bel Air, and the Belvedere trailed both in sales by wide margins, though it was still pretty popular with 51,266 built for 1951-52.

Chrysler didn't bother to separate 1951 from '52 production, partly because its cars changed so little. Plymouth was no exception, though a rear nameplate integrated with the trunk-handle assembly (replacing separate namescript) was a small spotter's point. Overdrive arrived as a new option, and all Plymouths continued with an important 1951 improvement: Oriflow shock absorbers, a Chrysler hydraulic type designed to improve ride and handling. But dumpy styling, a weak old six, and lack of full automatic transmission put Plymouth at a disadvantage in '52. Output sank by a substantial 204,000 units, aggravated by government-ordered civilian production cutbacks due to the Korean War.

The '53s addressed some of Plymouth's competitive deficits, starting with an outer-body reskin that brought flow-through fenderlines, one-piece windshield, and a

more aggressive grille. A single new 114-inch wheelbase was used for a revived two-series model group minus Concord (Cambridge expanded to embrace the business coupe and wagons). Another attempt to boost sales was the mid-year introduction of Hy-Drive, a manual transmission with torque converter that eliminated shifting between second and third, though you still had to clutch for first-gear starts.

But the '53s still looked stubby, and this continued for 1954, when Plymouth suffered from uninspired styling as much as any Chrysler make. Volume dwindled from the previous year's 650,000-plus to around 463,000, less than half of Ford/Chevy output. Models regrouped again, this time into cheap Plaza, mid-line Savoy, and top-shelf Belvedere series covering a $1600-$2300 price spread. Plaza and Savoy each listed a club coupe, sedans with two or four doors, and a Suburban, wagon; there was also a Plaza business coupe. Belvedere comprised four-door sedan, convertible, Suburban, and Sport Coupe hardtop.

Two important mechanical changes occurred during '54. The old six was enlarged for the first time since 1942, a longer stroke lifting displacement to 230.2 cid (3.25 × 4.63) and horsepower to 110. Also at about mid-year came fully automatic two-speed PowerFlite transmission as a new option. It would prove very popular.

Plymouth repeated this basic lineup for 1955 but with a dramatic difference: all-new styling conceived by Chrysler design chief Virgil Exner and executed under his assistant, Maury Baldwin. Suddenly, Plymouths looked exciting. What's more, they had performance to match

1955 Plymouth Belvedere convertible coupe

1955 Plymouth Belvedere Sport Coupe hardtop

1955 Plymouth Belvedere four-door sedan

1956 Plymouth Plaza two-door sedan

courtesy of the first V-8 in Plymouth history—and with a new polyspherical head design to boost.

Called "Hy-Fire," this V-8 was an excellent overhead-valve unit in the small-block tradition begun with Studebaker's 232 of 1951. It premiered in two sizes: a 241 (3.44 × 3.25) with 157 bhp, and a 260 (3.56 × 3.25) delivering 167 bhp standard or 177 bhp with "Power-Pak" (four-barrel carb and dual exhausts). Outstanding features ran to lightweight aluminum pistons, aluminum carburetor, and chrome-plated top piston rings for longer life and better oil control. Tuning changes brought the old 230 six, now called "PowerFlow," to 117 bhp.

Other new Plymouth talking points for '55 included suspended foot pedals, tubeless tires, front shocks enclosed within the front coil springs, and dashboard

lever control for the PowerFlite automatic. There were also several options new to this make: factory air conditioning, power windows, and power front seat.

But the most visible attraction was Plymouth's crisp new '55 styling, with pointed front and rear fenders, smooth flanks, a shapely tail, and a bright but not gaudy grille. Two-toning was confined to the roof and, via optional moldings, broad bodyside sweep panels. Four-door wagons were reinstated as Plaza and Belvedere Suburbans. The line-topping Belvedere convertible came only with V-8, as it would through the end of the decade.

Ads proclaimed the '55 a "great new car for the young in heart." It was certainly a clean break from Plymouth's plodding past. Though customers rushed to buy, production lagged and Plymouth dropped to sixth with only

1956 Plymouth Belvedere convertible coupe

1956 Plymouth Fury hardtop coupe

1957 Plymouth Fury hardtop coupe

1957 Plymouth Savoy two-door sedan

1958 Plymouth Suburban DeLuxe four-door station wagon

1958 Plymouth Savoy Sport Coupe hardtop

1959 Plymouth Sport Fury hardtop coupe

401,000 units. But for calendar '55 the division built a record 742,991 cars (including some '56s, of course)—a record that would stand well into the Sixties

Plymouth reclaimed fourth for 1956, which introduced "The Forward Look"—which mainly meant tailfins, achieved simply by raising rear fenderlines a little. Engineers simultaneously brought forth pushbutton PowerFlite, a 12-volt electrical system, and optional "Highway Hi-Fi," a record player that used special platters and a tone arm designed to stay in the groove (which it typically didn't on bumpy roads). Suburbans became a separate line with two-door Deluxe, two- and four-door Customs, and four-door Sport models respectively trimmed like Plaza, Savoy, and Belvedere. A Sport Sedan four-door hardtop expanded Belvedere models, and a two-door hardtop Savoy was added. Both Hy-Fire V-8s were larger and more potent, comprising a 270-cid base version (3.63 × 3.26) with 180 bhp, and a pair of 277s (3.75 × 3.13) packing 187 and 200 bhp.

An even hotter Plymouth arrived at mid-'56: the limited-edition Fury. An attractive hardtop coupe, it came only in white, set off by bodyside sweepspears of gold anodized aluminum. Power was supplied by a special 303 V-8 (3.82 × 3.31) with 240 bhp via 9.25:1 compression, solid lifters, stronger valve springs, dual exhausts, and Carter four-barrel carb. A stock Fury could do 0-60 mph in about 10 seconds and reach 110 mph, though one modified example approached 145 mph on the sands of Daytona Beach. The Fury gave a big boost to Plymouth's growing performance image, and 4485 of the '56s were sold—not bad for the $2866 price, some $600 above the Belvedere hardtop.

After record-shattering '56 production of nearly 553,000, Plymouth zoomed to better than 762,000 on the strength of its stunning, all-new '57 line. "Suddenly it's 1960," said the ads, and not without reason. Next to its rivals, Plymouth probably did seem "three full years ahead," with the lowest beltline and the highest tailfins of the traditional Low-Priced Three. Wheelbases stretched to 122 inches for wagons and to 118 inches on other models. Offerings were unchanged through mid-year, when a Savoy Sport Sedan hardtop was added.

The old "PowerFlow" six had been coaxed up to 132 bhp by now, and there were no fewer than five V-8s: 197- and 235-bhp 277s, new 301s (3.91 × 3.13) with 215/235 bhp, and the Fury's even larger new 318 (3.91 × 3.31) with 290 bhp. TorqueFlite, Chrysler's excellent new three-speed automatic, arrived as an optional alternative to PowerFlite. Also shared with other '57 Chrysler automobiles was torsion-bar front suspension, whose superior geometry made this the best-handling Plymouth in history.

It's hard to remember how truly different Plymouth seemed in '57: low and wide with distinctive shark fins; a graceful grille; a front bumper raised over a vertically slotted center panel; two-toning on roof and tasteful bodyside color panels (sometimes the roof alone); huge glass areas (the convertible windshield curved at the top as well as the sides); a delicate-looking thin-section roofline on hardtop coupes. Suburbans gained load space

1959 Plymouth Sport Fury hardtop coupe

1959 Plymouth Sport Fury convertible coupe

via an upright spare tire in the right rear fender, an idea borrowed from the 1956 Plymouth Plainsman show car. The '57s were indeed memorable, but their tendency to early rust—reflecting design flaws and a general decline in Chrysler's quality control that year—makes good examples fairly rare today.

A predictably mild facelift gave the '58s four headlamps, a horizontal-bar grille insert (repeated in the under-bumper modesty panel), and small round taillights at the base of the fins (bright metal filled the space above). A trio of 318 V-8s offered 225-290 bhp (the latter standard for Fury), and a newly optional 350 "Golden Commando" engine (4.06 × 3.38) delivered 305 bhp or, with that year's rare fuel-injection option, 315 bhp. A deep national recession limited production to just under 444,000.

Plymouth shared in the industry's modest '59 recovery, building a bit more than 458,000 cars that were more heavily restyled—and more heavy-handed: longer and higher fins, a garish eggcrate grille, headlamps with odd "siamesed" eyelids, more prominent bumpers, more plentiful bright trim. The Plaza vanished, Savoy and Belvedere moved down a notch, and Fury became a separate top-line series with two hardtops, four-door sedan, and convertible. Replacing the previous Fury as Plymouth's high performer was the Sport Fury, offering a convertible as well as hardtop coupe. Both cost around $3000 and carried a 260-bhp 318 V-8. The standard 318 delivered 230 bhp. Fuel injection was no more, but a new 361 Golden Commando with 305 bhp arrived.

Plymouth's '59 convertibles and hardtop coupes could be ordered with a simulated spare tire on the decklid, an add-on lump of tin reflecting Virgil Exner's love of "classic" design themes. It's since acquired the unflattering nickname of "toilet seat." Typical of the gimmick-mad Fifties—and increasingly of Chrysler—was the Sport Fury's standard "swivel-action" front seats: individual affairs (separated by a pull-down armrest) that turned outward at the touch of a lever to ease getting in and out. Sturdy latches kept them from swiveling while in use.

Also gimmicky, but occasionally predictive, were the several interesting Plymouth-branded show cars of this decade. They started with Ghia's 1951 XX-500, a pretty sedan that won Exner's patronage for the Italian coachworks to build later show cars and limousines. The 1954 Explorer, Ghia-built to Exner's design, was a smoothly styled grand tourer. Also in 1954, Briggs Manufacturing, the body maker that Chrysler purchased that year, contributed the two-seat Belmont roadster. It was supposed to spur Plymouth into offering something similar for the showroom—with Briggs-supplied bodies, of course—thus answering Chevy's Corvette and the Ford Thunderbird. A minuscule sports-car market precluded that idea, which was just as well: The Belmont wasn't much of a looker. The glassy '56 Plainsman, mentioned above, was followed by the even glassier 1958 Cabana "dream wagon," which sported four-door hardtop styling that would make it to showrooms on Chrysler's 1960-62 wagons, but not Plymouth's.

	PLYMOUTH AT A GLANCE									
Model Year	**1950**	**1951**	**1952**	**1953**	**1954**	**1955**	**1956**	**1957**	**1958**	**1959**
Price Range, $	1386-2387	1552-2237	1625-2344	1618-2220	1618-2288	1639-2425	1784-2866	1899-2925	2028-3067	2143-3131
Weight Range, Lbs.	2872-3353	2919-3294	2893-3256	2888-3193	2889-3186	3025-3475	3030-3650	3155-3840	3170-3840	3130-3805
Wheelbases, Ins.	111, 118.5	111, 118.5	111, 118.5	114	114	115	115	118, 122	118, 122	118, 122
6 Cyl. Engines, BHP	97	97	97	100	110	117	125	132	132	132
8 Cyl. Engines, BHP						157-177	180-240	197-290	225-315	230-305

1950 Pontiac Chieftain Eight DeLuxe convertible coupe

1950 Pontiac Streamliner Eight fastback four-door sedan

1950 Pontiac Chieftain Eight DeLuxe Catalina hardtop coupe

1951 Pontiac Chieftain Eight DeLuxe four-door sedan

1952 Pontiac Chieftain two-door sedan

1953 Pontiac Chieftain Custom Catalina hardtop coupe

Though not always obvious, Pontiac was a "senior Chevy" in the Fifties, much as it is today. It was born of Oakland in 1926 as part of an optimistic period expansion that also produced Cadillac's LaSalle, Buick's Marquette, and Oldsmobile's Viking as "companion makes" at General Motors. Pontiac would be the sole survivor. Marquette and Viking died swiftly in the Great Depression, while LaSalle was deemed unnecessary to Cadillac's continued survival after 1940. But Pontiac quickly outsold its parent, and displaced it entirely after 1931.

Settling in as the "step-up" make from Chevrolet, Pontiac occupied the second rung on the hugely successful price/prestige ladder conceived by legendary GM president Alfred P. Sloan. Though basic bodies and chassis were shared with Chevrolets, Pontiacs were typically bigger, brighter, and thus somewhat costlier. They also often boasted "senior GM" features Chevrolet didn't, such as fully automatic Hydra-Matic Drive, a new $185 option for 1948 that quickly rose to dominate Pontiac sales in the Fifties. Also, Chevy was limited to sixes through 1954, while Pontiac offered straight-eight models as well. These, too, came to so dominate sales that Pontiac would concentrate solely on the eight—a brand-new V-8—after 1954.

Pontiac fared very well in GM's corporate-wide postwar overhaul for 1949, gaining a new 120-inch-wheelbase chassis and an equally new A-body with smooth, attractive flush-fender styling created under the watchful eye of company design chief Harley Earl. The 1950 models were predictably quite similar. Offerings again included notchback Chieftain two- and four-door sedans and business and club coupes; a Chieftain convertible; and Streamliner four-door wagons and fastback two- and four-door sedans. Per established Pontiac custom, all came in six-

1952 Pontiac Chieftain sedan delivery

1953 Pontiac Chieftain sedan delivery

1954 Pontiac Chieftain DeLuxe two-door sedan

1954 Pontiac Star Chief Custom Catalina hardtop coupe

1954 Pontiac Star Chief Custom Catalina hardtop coupe

1955 Pontiac Star Chief Custom Safari two-door station wagon

and eight-cylinder versions with choice of standard and DeLuxe appointments, save the DeLuxe-only ragtop. A significant new entry was Pontiac's first hardtop-convertible, called Catalina, a Chieftain available in DeLuxe or new Super trim. By year's end, Catalinas accounted for some nine percent of total sales.

"Silver Streak" hood and rear-deck trim remained a Pontiac hallmark in 1950—a literal bright idea first applied by stylist Franklin Q. Hershey back in 1934. Also still much in evidence was the countenance of Chief Pontiac as a hood ornament; like many such devices of the day, it glowed when the headlights were on. There was no need to alter the basic year-old '49 styling, but Pontiac's 1950 "face" gained prominent vertical "teeth," and some trim was shuffled.

Pontiac's two inline L-head engines of this period also dated from the Thirties: long-stroke designs that were

long on stamina if short on excitement. For 1950, the eight was bored out from 248.9 to 268.4 cubic inches (3.38 × 3.75) good for 108 bhp standard or 113 with optional high-compression head. Pontiac's six remained at 239.2 cid (3.56 × 4.00), a size introduced back in 1941, but was offered in only one version with 90 bhp.

Postwar inflation was pushing Pontiac prices upward, and the 1950 line spanned a wide $1700-$2400 range. Nevertheless, Pontiac scored higher sales for the second straight year, smashing its 1941 model-year production record with nearly 466,500. Even so, the division still ranked fifth in the industry, and would remain so all the way through 1958.

Volume sank to about 370,000 for 1951 as all Detroit began feeling the effects of the Korean War, yet that total was Pontiac's second-best ever. Fastbacks were fading from favor, so the Streamliner four-door was dropped,

1955 Pontiac Star Chief convertible coupe

1956 Pontiac Star Chief convertible coupe

1956 Pontiac Star Chief Custom Safari two-door station wagon

1957 Pontiac Star Chief convertible coupe

followed in the spring of '51 by the two-door "sedan coupe." The most noticeable styling change was a "gull-wing" main grille bar situated below a prominent medallion. Both engines were tweaked, the six to 102 bhp, the eight to 122 bhp.

A busier grille and deletion of the long-deck Chieftain coupes were the main alterations for 1952. Government-ordered limits on civilian production combined with a nationwide steel strike to end Pontiac's model-year output at 271,000.

A major reskin of the '49 A-body and a two-inch longer wheelbase gave 1953's new all-Chieftain line a more "important" look. Sales trends had prompted these and other changes. Catalina hardtops, for example, now regularly took over 20 percent of total division sales, and Hydra-Matic installations were up to 84 percent. The '53s were thus larger in most every dimension, and shinier. Highlighting the new look were kicked-up rear fenders, a lower grille, more prominent bumpers, and a one-piece windshield.

Newly optional power steering made the '53s easier to park; more horsepower made them faster, especially the six. The latter now delivered 115 bhp with manual transmission or 118 with Hydra-Matic; corresponding eight-cylinder outputs were 118/122. A lowish rear axle ratio of 3.03:1 was specified for smooth top-range performance with Hydra-Matic. A mid-1953 fire at the Hydra-Matic plant shortened supplies, however, so about 18,500 Pontiacs were fitted with Chevrolet Powerglide in 1953-54. Pontiac sold extremely well for 1953: nearly 419,000 units.

Nineteen fifty-four brought a minor facelift of 1953's major one. Revised side moldings and a narrow oval in the central grille bar were the main distinctions. The big news, however, was Star Chief, a top-line eight-cylinder hardtop, convertible, and four-door sedan on a new 124-inch wheelbase. They were the plushest Pontiacs yet—and the priciest ($2300-$2600)—another sign of the division's steady drive upmarket. Star Chiefs sold well, but Pontiac's total volume slipped to just below 288,000, suggesting it was time for something new.

Which is just what Pontiac delivered for 1955. Among a claimed 109 new features were fully up-to-date styling, an improved chassis, and—the really hot item—the make's first modern overhead-valve V-8. The last, dubbed "Strato Streak," arrived with 287.2 cid (3.75 × 3.25), but would soon grow much larger. Standard horsepower was a flashing 180; an optional four-barrel carburetor yielded an even 200. A strong oversquare design with five main bearings, the Strato-Streak was somewhat related to Chevy's all-new 1955 "Turbo-Fire" V-8. Though not quite as advanced, it would serve Pontiac admirably for more than a quarter-century.

As on GM's other '55s, Pontiac styling was somewhat boxier but quite trendy, with wraparound windshield, cowl ventilation, new solid colors and two-tones, and a longer, lower look despite unchanged wheelbases. A blunt face was the one dubious aspect. As ever, this completely new A-body was shared with Chevrolet. Pontiac's

1957 Pontiac Bonneville convertible coupe

1957 Pontiac Star Chief Custom Catalina hardtop sedan

1958 Pontiac Star Chief Custom Catalina hardtop coupe

1958 Pontiac Bonneville Custom convertible coupe

shorter chassis still carried two Chieftain series, only now they were all V-8s: low-priced "860" and mid-range "870" sedans and wagons, plus "870" Catalina hardtop. Star Chief returned on its extended chassis with a base-trim sedan and convertible and a Custom Catalina and sedan.

Riding the Chieftain wheelbase but officially a Star Chief was the exotic Custom Safari, a hardtop-styled two-door wagon based on Chevrolet's new 1955 Bel Air Nomad. Chevy stylist Carl Renner recalled that "when Pontiac saw [the Nomad] they felt they could do something with it...Management wanted it for the Pontiac line, so it worked out." Like Nomad, the '55 Safari would continue with successive facelifts only through 1957 (after which both names were applied to conventional four-door wagons). Safaris naturally cost more than Nomads—$2962 at first—and thus sold in fewer numbers: 3760 for '55, 4042 for '56, and just 1292 of the '57s.

On balance, 1955 was a vintage year for Pontiac. Its cars were a solid hit with dealers and public alike, and the division built close to 554,000 of them, a new record. But some rough times lay ahead, and Pontiac wouldn't exceed this figure until 1963, after which it began setting new records. At least three factors accounted for this interim slump. Buick's Special and the base Olds 88 were more aggressively priced; demand for lower-medium cars shrank as import sales expanded in the late Fifties; and the 1956-58 Pontiacs weren't that exciting, though they were competitive in most ways and faster than ever.

The '56s were modestly facelifted, and new four-door Catalina hardtops were added to each series. Styling was less distinctive (tester Tom McCahill said the '56 looked like "it had been born on its nose"), and Pontiac had become known as a not-so-easy rider. A bore job took the

V-8 to 316.6 cid (3.94 × 3.25), but didn't yield a lot of extra power: only up to 205 in Chieftains and 227 bhp in Star Chiefs. Like most other makes, Pontiac settled for '56 volume that was well down on record-shattering '55, declining to 405,500 units and a sixth-place industry finish.

July 1956 ushered in a new general manager who would prove crucial to Pontiac's near-term fortunes. He was Semon E. "Bunkie" Knudsen, son of Thirties division chief "Big Bill" Knudsen and the youngest leader in Pontiac history. GM brass told him to do what he could with existing products for '57. Bunkie hustled, instituting longer rear springs in rubber shackles; 14-inch wheels and tires (replacing 15-inchers); pedal parking brake; optional automatic antenna; and a V-8 stroked to 347 cid (3.94 × 3.56) for 252-290 bhp. Stylewise, the grille became a massive buck-tooth affair; two-toning switched from 1955-56's half-car pattern to bodyside sweepspears; and Bunkie did the unthinkable by banishing Silver Streak trim as old-hat (it did, after all, date from his dad's time). Series were reorganized into low-end Chieftain and new mid-price Super Chief on the short wheelbase, with Star Chief returning on the longer chassis.

But where Bunkie really got his way for '57 was the Bonneville, a fast and flashy new Star Chief-based convertible introduced at mid-model year. Delivering 300 bhp via fuel injection, hydraulic lifters, and racing cam, this $5782 limited edition was the costliest and fastest Pontiac yet—even faster with optional Tri-Power (three two-barrel carbs). A fuel-injected Bonnie was timed at 18 seconds in the standing quarter-mile; a Tri-Power car did it in 16.8.

Because it was basically a promotional piece, the '57 Bonneville saw only 630 copies. But it gave Pontiac a

1959 Pontiac Catalina convertible coupe

1959 Pontiac Bonneville Sport Coupe hardtop

whole new performance image even as the Auto Manufacturers Association came down against factory-sponsored racing. (Though several '57 Pontiacs did run with distinction in NASCAR, they were strictly private entries.) Yet the lack of racing publicity didn't hamper sales. While Chevy, Olds, and Buick all lost sales to '57 Chrysler rivals, Pontiac built some 333,500 cars to move within 51,000 units of fifth-place Olds.

An all-new body should have made the '58s even more popular, but a recession set in and held output to only 217,000 units. Unlike most GM cars that year, Pontiac was quite well styled, with a simpler, full-width grille, quad headlights, and wider, concave sidespears. Bodies were lower but not much longer or wider (wheelbases were unchanged). Model offerings now ran to no fewer than seven Catalina hardtops with two or four doors. Bonneville became a regular series, and sold about 12,000 convertibles and hardtop coupes. Another bore job took the V-8 to 370 cid (4.06 × 3.56) for four standard engines offering from 240 bhp in manual-shift Chieftains/Super Chiefs to 285 in automatic Star Chiefs and Bonnevilles. Optional across-the-board were a 300-bhp Tri-Power unit and a 310-bhp fuelie.

Then came the first Pontiacs to fully reflect the Bunkie Knudsen touch. The '59s were not just startlingly new; they established the performance pattern that would carry Pontiac to undreamed-of glory in the Sixties. Crisp styling on a brand-new A-body introduced the split grille theme that remains a division hallmark to this day, plus modest

twin-fin rear fenders and minimal side trim. Wheelbases were again unchanged, but the wheels were set further apart on a new "Wide-Track" chassis that made Pontiacs among the most roadable cars in America.

The V-8 was again enlarged, newly stroked to 389 cid (4.06 × 3.75)—a number destined for greatness. Horse-power ran from 315 with Tri-Power down to 245. There was also a detuned 215-bhp "Tempest 420E" for economy-minded buyers, capable of delivering up to 20 mpg with a delicate right foot. Ridding Pontiac of "that Indian concept" was still part of Bunkie's plan, so Chieftain and Super Chief gave way to a new Catalina series on the short wheelbase; Bonneville again shared the longer one with Star Chief, which would hang on a good long while. Bolstered by new Safari wagons and Vista hardtop sedans, the '59 Bonnevilles garnered some 82,000 sales. Total volume rose to near 383,000, boosting Pontiac into fourth place for the first time.

Pontiac's Fifties show cars were always interesting and often predictive. The smooth '54 Strato Streak previewed pillarless four-doors to come for '56. Also shown in '54 was the first Bonneville, an aggressive-looking two-seater with canopy-type cockpit on a 100-inch wheelbase. Both cars carried straight eights. The 1955 Strato Star was a two-door, four-seat hardtop that also forecast '56 styling. Wildest of all was the 1956 Club de Mer, with "twin pod" seating and dual bubble windshields. Standing only 38.4 inches high, its aluminum body was painted Cerulean blue, the favorite color of design domo Harley Earl.

PONTIAC AT A GLANCE										
Model Year	**1950**	**1951**	**1952**	**1953**	**1954**	**1955**	**1956**	**1957**	**1958**	**1959**
Price Range, $	1571-2411	1713-2629	1956-2446	1956-2664	1968-2630	2105-2962	2370-2857	2463-5782	2573-3586	2633-3532
Weight Range, Lbs.	3209-3689	3193-3698	3253-3688	3391-3716	3331-3776	3476-3791	3452-3797	3515-5425	3640-4065	3870-4370
Wheelbases, Ins.	120	120	120	122	122	122, 124	122, 124	122, 124	122, 124	122, 124
6 Cyl. Engines, BHP	90	96	100	115	115, 118					
8 Cyl. Engines, BHP	108	116	118	118	122, 127	180, 200	205, 227	252-310	240-310	215-315

Rambler, the successful compact begun by Nash in 1950, became a separate make after introducing larger four-door models for '55 and new styling for '56. These and subsequent Fifties events reflected the changing fortunes of American Motors Corporation after its formation in April 1954 with the Nash-Hudson merger instigated by Nash president George Mason.

It had long been Mason's dream to combine Nash with Hudson, then bring in Studebaker and Packard to form a single company enjoying the same economies of scale as the Big Three. Without combining, he reasoned, none of these independents could survive long-term. As a halfway measure he persuaded Packard president James Nance to take over ailing Studebaker, which was accomplished in 1954. But when Mason died suddenly that October, so did his dream of a "Big Fourth." His assistant, George Romney, became AMC president, forgot all about linking up with S-P, and bet the farm on Rambler.

It was all Romney could really do, but events worked in his favor. Rambler continued going from strength to strength, helped by the flash recession of 1958.

The 1957 Ramblers were continuations of the reskinned '56 models sold with Nash and Hudson badges. Besides new "R" hood medallions, cosmetic changes were limited to just slightly reshuffled trim and a T-shaped grille ornament in the space above the eggcrate section. The big news was power: AMC's 250-cid V-8 first introduced in 1956. Rated at 190 horsepower, it was available in four body styles, all unibody four-doors on the 108-inch wheelbase first seen for '55. Permutations involved sedans and Cross Country station wagons with and without B-pillars—making Rambler the first with hardtop wagons. As before, all offered a choice of Super and Custom trim. So did a parallel line of six-cylinder cars retaining the 195.6-cid familiar from Nash days. However, this was tweaked from 120 to 135 bhp. The six-cylinder line also included a downmarket Deluxe sedan, the price-leader at $1961.

These Ramblers were solid, reliable smaller cars that could be quite stylish with optional two-toning. As in the Nash era, "Continental kit" outside spare tires were available for sedans, and wagons featured a roll-down tailgate window instead of a clumsy liftgate, something Ford and GM wagons didn't have. "We just rolled with those cars," as future AMC chairman Roy D. Chapin, Jr., later recalled. "We couldn't get enough." Indeed, of the 118,900 AMC cars built in calendar '57, all but 7816 were Ramblers. The rest, of course, were Nashes and Hudsons, which would not return for '58—at least not exactly.

Romney liked to assail Detroit's "gas-guzzling dinosaurs" while preaching Rambler's smaller-is-better virtues. All the more surprising, then, that AMC had a performance Rambler for 1957. This was an interesting Custom Country Club four-door hardtop aptly branded Rebel. Arriving at midyear with flashes of anodized aluminum on its sides, the Rebel came with the same 255-bhp 327 V-8 (4.00 × 3.25) that powered that year's final Nashes and Hudsons, but was much quicker by virtue of lower weight. The extra power made the Rebel more of a

1956 Rambler Super four-door sedan

1956 Rambler Custom Cross Country four-door station wagon

1957 Rambler Rebel Custom hardtop sedan

1958 Rambler Ambassador four-door hardtop station wagon

1959 Rambler Ambassador four-door sedan

handler than other Ramblers, so AMC specified standard Gabriel shocks, front anti-roll bar, heavy-duty springs, power steering, and power brakes. Performance was impressive, let alone for a Rambler. During tests at Daytona Beach, a Rebel flew from 0 to 60 mph—and 50 to 80—in scarcely more than seven seconds.

Not that it mattered much. With 9.75:1 compression, the Rebel demanded premium fuel and drank a fair bit of it, which hardly appealed to Rambler's economy-conscious market. As a result, only 1500 were built. Then too, the Rebel was the most expensive '57 Rambler at $2786.

Meantime, economy imports were fast-climbing the sales charts, led by VW's already antiquated Beetle. Accordingly, AMC made a bold move for '58 by bringing back the 100-inch-wheelbase Rambler two-door sedan from 1955—the first, and so far only, revival of its kind. Renamed Rambler American, it wore a new mesh-type grille and exposed rear wheels. DeLuxe and Super versions were offered along with a stripped business model, all at very low prices: $1790-$1875. At that level the American couldn't help but sell, and over 42,000 were registered for the 12 months.

Regular Ramblers weren't ignored for 1958, receiving more than 100 changes, including a complete outer-body reskin that made them look slightly bulkier on unchanged wheelbases. Hardtop wagons were omitted, but dual headlamps (returned to the fenders) and little canted tailfins served fashion. A pedal-type parking brake served function. AMC even adopted *de rigueur* pushbuttons to control the optional Borg-Warner "Flash-O-Matic" self-shift transmission. Though V-8 models were now called Rebel, they retained the 250 engine, which was booted to 215 bhp. The six-cylinder cars, now with 127 or 138 bhp, were still nameless—and again far more popular, no real surprise.

What was surprising, other than the American, was a new 117-inch-wheelbase line called Rambler Ambassador, though brochures implied you should think of it as a distinct make ("Ambassador by Rambler"). No matter. This was simply the 108-inch-wheelbase design with nine extra inches grafted on ahead of the cowl, plus a standard four-barrel 327 V-8 with 270 bhp. Offerings comprised the usual four-door sedans, Country Club hardtop sedans, and pillared and pillarless Cross Country wagons in

Super and Custom trim. In appearance, these Ambassadors were nothing like their Nash forebears and everything like regular '58 Ramblers. The only differences were nameplates, a fine-checked grille, broad swathes of anodized aluminum on Customs, plusher interiors, and arguably better proportions from the longer hood.

It's interesting that the '58 Ambassador virtually matched combined '57 Nash/Hudson volume, production ending at 14,570 for the model year. Rarest of the breed, at just 294 units, was the Custom Cross Country hardtop wagon, the only such model in AMC's '58 line. Despite that mild disappointment, AMC's total '58 production was almost double its '57 output: 186,277 units.

AMC stayed with this winning formula for 1959 to net $60 million in profits on volume of nearly 374,420—a new record for the fledgling firm. Ramblers and Ambassadors received more complicated body trim, plus a beltline curved up gently at the rear doors to blend more smoothly into the fins. Ambassadors also got a more ornate grille with prominent "floating" horizontal bar.

But the swing to compacts was on, and both the American and cheaper standard Ramblers had new competition in Studebaker's pert '59 Lark. Perhaps anticipating this, AMC revived its old two-door 100-inch-wheelbase wagon to bolster this year's American sedans. Offered in DeLuxe and Super versions, the wagon helped the littlest Rambler rack up 90,000 model-year sales.

The bigger Ramblers also did very well in 1959's modest industry-wide recovery. Ambassador volume took a satisfying leap to 23,769, and standard Ramblers attracted over a quarter-million sales.

In all, AMC's 1957-59 sales performance represented a remarkable comeback from nail-biting 1954-56. And the good times would keep rolling for the next few years. Rambler almost beat Plymouth for third place on the 1960 volume roster, then actually did it for 1961. But Romney left soon afterwards (to become governor of Michigan), by which time the Big Three were seriously eroding Rambler's market with compacts of their own. Under new president Roy Abernethy, AMC's response was to compete with the Big Three in every market sector, but Kenosha's David was too small to do really well against the Detroit Goliaths. Thus began a long downhill slide from which AMC would never quite recover.

RAMBLER AT A GLANCE										
Model Year	1950	1951	1952	1953	1954	1955	1956	1957	1958	1959
Price Range, $							1829-2494	1961-2786	1775-3116	1821-3116
Weight Range, Lbs.							2891-3110	2911-3409	2439-3586	2435-3591
Wheelbases, Ins.							108	108	100-117	100-117
6 Cyl. Engines, BHP							120	125, 135	90-138	90-138
8 Cyl. Engines, BHP								190, 255	215, 270	215, 270

America's oldest maker of wheeled vehicles was 98 years young in 1950—and having one of its best years with cars, building 320,884. Grand preparations were underway to kick off Studebaker's upcoming "second century," about which there were many equally grand predictions.

But that second century was cut far short. Within 14 years, Studebaker would flee the U.S. to concentrate production in Canada, where the last Studebakers were built two years later.

Three factors figure in Studebaker's ultimate demise. First, the firm suffered lower productivity than rival automakers, even though its workers were among the best paid. Second, Studebaker's huge old South Bend plant was not only a high-overhead facility, but more isolated from component suppliers than were Michigan factories. Third, Studebaker and other independents were severely wounded by the Ford/GM price wars of the mid-Fifties. With lower volumes, the smaller companies couldn't afford to discount as much, and sales suffered accordingly.

A fourth factor may have been bad timing. Studebaker was "first by far with a postwar car," the all-new 1947 models with Raymond Loewy's smooth, envelope-bodied "Which Way Is It Going?" look. But hindsight shows that the rabid postwar seller's market didn't demand new designs, just new cars. Thus, Studebaker could have stayed longer with prewar models and held back all-postwar designs until 1949 or '50—as indeed most all the majors did.

As it was, Studebaker didn't field a replacement until 1953, by which time its '47 design was six years on the market and quite dated. This very likely cost Studebaker some buyers—and there's an old business axiom that says once customers are lost, they're very hard to get back.

The 1950 Studebakers were essentially the 1947-49 models facelifted from the cowl forward. According to Bob Bourke, chief of the Loewy team that designed Studebakers from the late Thirties, the new "bullet nose" front was ordered by the French-speaking Loewy with the words, "Now Bob, eet has to look like zee aeroplane." It did, giving 1950 Studebakers the most bizarre face of any American car since Graham's abortive 1939-40 "Sharknose." Studebaker called its styling "The Next Look," but nobody copied it, though it sort of forecast the later vertical grille motifs of Edsel and Pontiac.

The new front also increased wheelbase a nominal one inch for all 1950 Studebakers, which again divided between Champions and Commanders on new respective spans of 113 and 120 inches. Both series retained familiar six-cylinder Studebaker power. Champions carried a 1939-vintage 169.6 cubic-inch unit (bore and stroke: 3.00×4.00 inches) with 85 horsepower; Commanders again used a 245.6-cid engine (3.31×4.75) with 102 bhp. Each line again included DeLuxe and Regal DeLuxe two- and four-door sedans and five-passenger Starlight club coupes, plus Regal convertible. Champion added three-passenger coupes with very blind rear roof quarters, and a quartet of cheap closed Customs starting in the low

1950 Studebaker Commander Regal DeLuxe convertible coupe

1952 Studebaker Champion DeLuxe coupe

1953 Studebaker Commander Starliner hardtop coupe

$1400s. Exclusive to Commander was the Land Cruiser, a lushly trimmed sedan on a unique 124-inch chassis, priced at $2187. The big mechanical news for 1950 was fully automatic transmission as a new option. An excellent Studebaker unit aptly termed "Automatic Drive," it was designed in cooperation with the Detroit Gear Division of Borg-Warner.

Wheelbases were again rearranged for 1951, with Champs and Commanders on an abbreviated 115-inch spread; Land Cruiser was demoted to its own 119-inch platform. Champion power was unchanged, but Commanders were treated to Studebaker's first V-8. Displacing 232.6 cubic inches (3.38×3.25), it pumped out 120 bhp by conventional means, though overhead cams and hemispherical combustion chambers had been considered.

The 232 and its later evolutions have been called heavy for their displacements, but that's only compared with similar engines developed after significant improvements occurred in casting and foundry techniques. In fact, this

1954 Studebaker Champion DeLuxe Conestoga two-door station wagon

1955 Studebaker President Speedster hardtop coupe

1956 Studebaker Sky Hawk hardtop coupe

1956 Studebaker President Classic four-door sedan

1957 Studebaker Golden Hawk hardtop coupe

V-8 was the first of many robust, efficient American small-blocks under 300 cid, and the subsequent Dodge, Ford, Chevrolet, and Plymouth V-8s certainly benefited from its technology. Perhaps the 232's greatest contribution was to close the power gap between low-priced and high-priced cars.

Rising production costs forced Studebaker to raise prices a bit for 1951, but buyers seemed happy to pay for the lively V-8, which boosted Commander sales by no less than 50 percent. Though not a powerhouse, the V-8 did give up to 100 mph flat out, plus 0-60 times of just under 13 seconds. As time would tell, this engine would stand a good deal more displacement and power.

Styling changes were slight. The bullet nose was toned down by painting its chrome outer ring, the prominent air vents above the grille were erased, and model names were spelled out on the leading edge of the hood. However you think it looks now, the 1950-51 Studebaker was quite saleable. But Korean War restrictions helped hold 1951 car production to 268,585. Despite this, South Bend actually increased its market share from 4.02 to 4.17 percent.

An all-new Studebaker was planned for centennial 1952, with unit construction and evolutionary bullet-nose styling. But though this "N-Series" progressed to a running prototype, it was abandoned due to continuing government restraints on civilian production and a big upturn in Studebaker's military business.

Accordingly, the '47 platform was facelifted for one last time, gaining a low, toothy full-width grille often called the "clam digger." Offerings stood pat save the belated addition of new Starliner hardtop coupes. As in '51, trim levels were Custom, DeLuxe, and Regal for Champion, Regal and State for Commander. Starliners were top-liners. To no one's surprise, Studebaker paced the 1952 Indy 500, and a Champ and Commander scored class wins in the Mobilgas Economy Run. But South Bend's centennial was spoiled by much lower car production of 186,239 units, though that wasn't so surprising either, given the old basic design.

Studebaker took care of that in literal high style for the first model year of its second century. Headlining the all-new '53 lineup were the now-legendary "Loewy coupes": sleek, low, and clean—triumphs of good taste. There were six in all: pillarless Regal Starliners and pillared Deluxe and Regal Starlights, Commander, and Champion. Despite the "Loewy" nickname, the basic design was actually shaped by Bob Bourke. Though first intended only for a show car, Loewy convinced Studebaker managers to commit to production. It would have looked smashing as a convertible, but Studebaker sadly never got around to one.

Mounting the new 120.5-inch Land Cruiser wheelbase rather than the 116.5-inch span used for other '53s, the Loewy coupes were perfect from every angle. Rightly advertised as the "new European look," it's still widely regarded as America's best automotive design of the decade. That year's two- and four-door sedans were almost as pretty, bearing general coupe lines but necessarily stubbier and more upright on the shorter wheelbase.

Alas, tooling the '53 line delayed its production, which ended at a disappointing 169,599. When things finally did get rolling, demand for coupes promptly ran four times that for sedans. Management had expected just the reverse, and both time and sales were lost in switching around. For all that, Studebaker managed a slim $2.69 million profit.

Eggcrate grille inserts identified the '54 Studebakers, which again included "Loewys," a pair of cheap Champ Custom sedans, and Deluxe and Regal sedans in each series. A newcomer was the two-door all-steel Conestoga, South Bend's first station wagon. Named for the famous "prairie schooners" of Studebaker's infancy, it came as Deluxe and Regal Champs and Commanders. Also new for '54 were seven extra horses for Commanders and larger brakes across the board.

But Studebaker's weaknesses were now painfully apparent. Bourke "priced out" a Commander Starliner using the General Motors cost structure, and found that Chevrolet could have sold it for $1900; Studebaker charged $2500. Meanwhile, the "Ford Blitz" was on, as Dearborn waged a price war with GM. Though neither giant damaged the other, they wreaked havoc on the independents, and Studebaker's model-year volume plunged to 81,930.

Just when things looked blackest, Packard bought Studebaker in October 1954, ushering in Packard's able James J. Nance as president of the new Studebaker-Packard Corporation. But this alliance, as one executive later admitted, was like "two drunks trying to help each other across the road." It would prove poisonous to Packard, which would be killed off in 1958.

Meantime, Studebaker hitched hopes for higher sales to a group of facelifted '55s laden with chrome. Among them were new top-line Presidents (reviving a grand prewar name): Deluxe and State four-door sedans (replacing Land Cruiser) and pillared and pillarless State coupes. More power was the order of the day. The Champ six grew to 185.6 cid (3.00 × 4.38) and 101 bhp; the Commander V-8 was pumped up to 140 bhp despite being downsized to 224.3 cid (3.56 × 2.81). Presidents carried a new 259 V-8 (3.56 × 3.25) delivering 175 bhp. Seeking to

hold production costs, Studebaker discarded its own automatic transmission for the cheaper "Flight-O-Matic" from Borg-Warner.

But sales still lagged, so in January '55 the Commander was promoted to a 162-bhp "Bearcat" 259 (an optional "High Power Kit" added 20 bhp more), and Presidents got a 185-bhp "Passmaster" version. At the same time, non-coupe Presidents and Commanders gained trendy "Ultra Vista" wrapped windshields, and a jazzy President Speedster hardtop bowed with special "quilted" leather interior, full instrumentation in a tooled-metal dash, and wild two-tone combinations like pink and black or "lemon and lime." But at $3253, the Speedster was not a big seller (just 2215 built). Neither were its linemates. In a year when most makes set new sales records, Studebaker managed only 133,826 cars. At this point, South Bend needed about 250,000 annual sales just to break even.

Gamely, Studebaker reskinned for '56, achieving a squarer look announced by large mesh-filled grilles. Commander and Champion gained cheap two-door "sedanets" priced under $2000, a spiffy long-chassis Classic sedan joined the President range at $2489, and wagons became a separate series with new names: Pelham (Champion), Parkview (Commander), and Pinehurst (President).

Coupes were also split off to create a new Hawk line of "family sports cars." These were the last Fifties Studebakers styled by the Loewy team, who conjured an admirably restrained facelift of the 1953-54 coupe, adding modest tailfins and a large square grille riding high on an elevated hood. Deluxe interiors featured tooled-metal dash trim, as on the '55 Speedster. There were four versions: pillared Flight Hawk and Power Hawk and hardtop Sky Hawk and Golden Hawk. All were good-looking, competent on curves, and impressive on straights.

Topping Studebaker's '56 engine chart was a 275-bhp 352 V-8 from new partner Packard, exclusive power for the Golden Hawk. Champs, Flight Hawk, and Pelham wagon used an unchanged six, while 259 V-8s now delivered 170/185 bhp in Commander/Power Hawk/ Parkview. A new 289 (3.56 × 3.63) offered 195/210/225 bhp in Presidents/Sky Hawk/Pinehurst.

The Flight Hawk listed below $2000, the Golden Hawk

1958 Studebaker Champion four-door sedan

1958 Studebaker Scotsman two-door sedan

1959 Studebaker Lark DeLuxe two-door station wagon

at $3061, so Studebaker's "family sports cars" were good buys. Alas, they were peripheral sellers appealing mainly to enthusiasts, and the bread-and-butter '56s appealed to few mainstream buyers. As a result, Studebaker managed just 85,462 cars, including 19,165 Hawks. And things would get worse: In 1957-58, Studebaker and Packard combined couldn't sell more than 70,000 cars a year.

In May 1956, S-P president James Nance arranged with Curtiss-Wright Corporation, through its president, Roy Hurley, for "advisory management services" to S-P—which meant a cash bailout. Plans for an expansive new '57 S-P line were abruptly canceled, and Nance resigned along with Studebaker chairman Paul Hoffman and president Harold Vance. This left Hurley to preside over a group of 1957-58 Studebakers facelifted in the only possible way: on the cheap.

Duncan McRae did the deed, giving standard '57s a full-width grille and grossly distended rear fenders suggesting fins. Hawks gained more prominent fins that didn't seriously detract from overall appearance. Models were cut to Deluxe and Custom Champ and Commander sedans, Pelham and Parkview wagons, three Presidents, the Golden Hawk, and a new pillared Silver Hawk available with six or 289 V-8. Somehow, Studebaker also managed four-door wagons: Commander Provincial and President Broadmoor. Higher compression lifted the 259 V-8 to 180/195 bhp, and the Golden Hawk exchanged its Packard engine for a Studebaker 289 with Paxton supercharger that developed the same 275 bhp. Another attempt to spark sales produced the midyear Scotsman, a

wagon and two sedans offering six-cylinder power but very little else for well under $2000. Though some 9300 were sold, overall '57 sales did not spark, production falling to 74,738.

The '58s were uglier still, with hastily contrived four-headlamp fronts and even more garish trim. Commander and President offered new Starlight hardtop coupes on the 116.5-inch chassis, but the overall lineup was thinner, as were engine choices (down to the six, 180-bhp 259, and three 289s). The Scotsman did well in that recession year with nearly 21,000 sales. A good thing, too, for total volume dropped again, this time to 62,114.

Studebaker might have died right there had it not been for the successful compact Lark of 1959. Replacing all the old standard models, Lark retained the basic sedan/wagon inner structure of 1953-58, but was shorn of all the extra sheetmetal hung on over the years—and with it, up to 200 pounds in curb weight. In its place, McRae applied simple, clean, well-formed styling announced by a return to dual headlamps and a Hawk-type grille. The 169.6-cid six also returned, making 90 bhp in "Lark VI" Deluxe and Regal two- and four-door sedans, two-door wagons, and Regal hardtop coupe. A Regal four-door, hardtop, and wagon comprised the "Lark VIII" series with standard two-barrel 180-bhp 259 V-8; optional four-barrel carb and dual exhaust added 15 horses. Wagons rode the familiar 113-inch wheelbase, but other Larks sat on a trim new 108.5-inch chassis.

With all this, the Lark was lively yet economical and surprisingly roomy. Aided by starting prices below $2000, it was a smash hit, garnering 131,078 sales.

Studebaker hadn't given up on "family sports cars," but there was only one pillared V-8 Silver Hawk for '59. Available with both 259 Lark engines, it added only 7788 units to total model-year production.

Nevertheless, the Lark led Studebaker out of the financial woods, and South Bend recorded its first profit in six years. Yet barely four years later, Studebaker was back in trouble—and for the same reasons: insufficient sales to cover development costs for new models to replace increasingly unpopular old ones. Thus were the last Studebakers built in 1966. Losing Studebaker was a shame, but it was, perhaps, inevitable.

STUDEBAKER AT A GLANCE										
Model Year	**1950**	**1951**	**1952**	**1953**	**1954**	**1955**	**1956**	**1957**	**1958**	**1959**
Price Range, $	1419-2328	1561-2481	1735-2548	1735-2374	1758-2556	1741-3253	1844-3060	1776-3182	1795-3282	1925-2590
Weight Range, Lbs.	2620-3375	2585-3240	2655-3230	2690-3180	2705-3265	2740-3275	2780-3395	2725-3415	2695-3470	2577-3148
Wheelbases, Ins.	113-124	115, 119	115, 119	116.5, 120.5	116.5, 120.5	116.5, 120.5	116.5, 120.5	116.5, 120.5	116.5, 120.5	108.5-120.5
6 Cyl. Engines, BHP	85, 102	85	85	85	85	101	101	101	101	90
8 Cyl. Engines, BHP		120	120	120	120	140, 175	195-275	180-275	180-275	180-195

Willys-Overland built passenger cars for nearly 35 years before it ever built a Jeep, and some of those years were sensational. In 1928, for example, W-O ran third in industry production (315,000), right behind Chevy and Ford. But that would be the peak. Willys quickly withered in the Depression, and a desperate turn to four-cylinder compacts failed to restore financial health. But the Jeep did. Willys thus entered peacetime inextricably linked to the heroic little military vehicle beloved by millions of GIs.

It made sense to keep a good thing going in the early postwar years, so Willys delayed new passenger models in favor of Jeep-based products. These included the inevitable civilian version of the military Jeep, plus two hybrids. The first was a station wagon introduced in 1946 and destined to live for 20 years. Though usually considered a truck and not a car, it arguably qualifies as the first modern all-steel wagon.

More directly automotive was the Jeepster, a jaunty open tourer designed during wartime by Brooks Stevens, who also did the wagon. Announced in 1948, the Jeepster offered seating for four on the 104-inch wagon wheelbase, plus a manual soft top and a 63-horsepower 134.3-cubic-inch four-cylinder engine (bore and stroke: 3.13 × 4.38 inches), a holdover from Willys' final 1941-42 "Americar" passenger models. Six-cylinder Jeepsters arrived for 1949, with 148.5 cid (3.00 × 3.50) and 72 bhp. Both engines were switched from L-head to overhead-valve F-head design by 1950, when an eggcrate grille replaced vertical slats, trim became somewhat less deluxe, and the six was enlarged to 161 cid (3.13 × 4.38), good for 75 bhp.

Priced in the $1400-$1500 range, the Jeepster was quite popular for such a specialized product. First-year sales were strong: 10,326. But this evidently satisfied the market, for 1949 production totaled just 2960. The 1950 figure was a healthier 5844, but some were unsold at year's end and registered as '51 models.

Willys could likely have lived just fine on Jeep, Jeep wagons, trucks, and military vehicles. But the high optimism of the early postwar period made returning to cars seem a no-lose proposition. After entertaining numerous proposals, president Ward Canaday selected a trim 108-inch-wheelbase unitized design engineered by the distinguished Clyde Paton and styled by the inventive Phil Wright. By 1952 it was ready for the road, trumpeted as "The Revolutionary New Aero-Willys."

It was a fine effort: fashionably square and slab-sided, relatively light (2500-2600 pounds), roomy, and blessed with good handling. There were four models: a hardtop coupe called Aero-Eagle, plus three two-door sedans. The Aero-Lark used the 75-bhp 161 six from late Jeepsters. Aero-Wing and Aero-Ace sedans and the Eagle hardtop ran the overhead-valve version with 90 bhp. Though small, the 161s delivered good performance, plus fuel economy on the order of 25 miles per gallon.

But high price proved an immediate sales problem. For example, the $2155 Eagle hardtop cost $150 more than Chevrolet's "full-size" Bel Air, while the bare-bones Aero-Lark cost $24 more than a two-door Chevy DeLuxe.

1950 Willys Jeepster phaeton convertible

1952 Willys Aero-Wing two-door sedan

1954 Willys Aero-Eagle Custom hardtop coupe

1954 Willys Aero-Ace DeLuxe four-door sedan

1955 Willys Bermuda hardtop coupe

1955 Willys Bermuda hardtop coupe

Willys dealers were thus hard pressed to explain not only how the Jeep people could produce a smooth, comfortable family car, but why they had to charge so much for it. Still, 1952-model production was good, if not great: 31,363. The mid-range Aero-Wing accounted for well over a third.

Offerings expanded for 1953, when appearance changed only in detail—notably red hubcap emblems and a gold-plated "W" in the grille, honoring Willys's 50th anniversary. About 500 Aero-Larks were built for export with the old F-head fours, but engines were otherwise unchanged. Aero-Wing was replaced by Aero-Falcon, and a new four-door sedan was developed in Lark, Falcon, and Ace versions. The hardtop Eagle was again rather pricey, though up only $2 from '52. Helped by the end of the Korean War and government curbs on civilian production, Willys had another modestly good year, selling about 42,000 units.

But then Willys-Overland was purchased in 1954 by Henry Kaiser, who combined it with his ailing Kaiser-Frazer to form Toledo-based Kaiser-Willys Sales Corporation. K-F sold its sprawling Willow Run, Michigan, plant, near Ypsilanti, to General Motors (which still uses it), and Kaiser production was shifted to the old Willys plant.

This takeover did not immediately affect the '54 Aero-Willys, which was little more than a '53 with larger tail-lights and revised interior. But March 1954 brought a raft of changes. Chief among them was Kaiser's 226-cid L-head six (3.31 × 4.38), which was shoehorned in as optional power for Ace and Eagle. There were also new Ace and Eagle Customs, basically the standard articles with "continental" spare tire.

Though heavier than the Willys 161, the Kaiser 226 brought a useful 25 extra horsepower that made the Aero relatively fast. Top speed was a little higher at 85 mph, but the big six dropped typical 0-60 mph times to around 14 seconds. As an experiment, a few Aeros were given 140-bhp supercharged Manhattan engines, which engineers say gave pickup comparable to that of contemporary V-8s engines.

All '54s handled much better than earlier Aeros, thanks to a new front end with threaded trunions adjustable for wear, stronger shocks and A-arms, and longer kingpins, coil springs, and steering idler arm. All new was a cross-member connecting the left and right front suspension assemblies, which reduced lateral torque shake and toe-in variations. The result was one of the best ride/handling combinations available in Fifties America. It made the Eagle hardtop even more attractive, but price was still a problem: now close to $2600 with optional GM Hydra-Matic. In all, the best Aero yet failed to convince many customers, and production dropped to 11,717.

By early 1955, Kaiser-Willys decided to abandon U.S. car production, but not before completing 5905 Willys models. No longer called Aero, the '55s comprised Custom two- and four-door sedans and a newly named Bermuda hardtop (née Eagle); Willys also built 659 Ace four-doors, mainly for export. Engine choices were not changed, but prices were: drastically cut in a last-ditch effort to attract sales. The Bermuda, for instance, was slashed to $1895, and was thus honestly advertised as America's lowest-priced hardtop.

Sales also prompted the ambitious '55 Willys facelift by Kaiser stylists Buzz Grisinger and Herb Weissinger, distinguished by a busy two-tier grille (replacing the simple horizontal bar of prior years) and Z-line side moldings that made for odd two-toning. A neat hardtop wagon had been planned for 1955-56, and designers Dutch Darrin and Duncan McRae worked up more ambitious restyles for the future. But Willys had no future, at least in passenger cars. So after 2215 final units, most powered by the 226 engine, Willys went back to making nothing but Jeeps.

But the Aero would live a good while longer in South America, where Kaiser's Willys do Brasil subsidiary eventually took over the Aero dies and offered a cleaned-up '55 with F-head Willys power from 1960 through '62. Designer Brooks Stevens then applied handsome new square-rigged outer panels, and the car continued all the way through 1972 as the Aero-Willys 2600, then Willys Itamaraty and finally *Ford* Itamaraty (Dearborn acquired Willys do Brasil through American Motors in 1967). That's eloquent testimony to the sound basic design of the original Aero-Willys. A pity it wasn't more appreciated by homefolks in the Fifties.

WILLYS AT A GLANCE						
Model Year	**1950**	**1951**	**1952**	**1953**	**1954**	**1955**
Price Range, $	1494-1690	1597-1703	1731-2155	1646-2157	1737-2411	1725-1895
Weight Range, Lbs.	2392-2485	2459-2485	2487-2584	2487-2575	2623-2904	2751-2847
Wheelbases, Ins.	104	104	108	108	108	108
4 Cyl. Engines, BHP	63, 72	72		72	72	
6 Cyl. Engines, BHP	70, 75	75	75, 90	75, 90	90-115	90-115

Carmakers and independent sources treat automotive production in both *model* years and *calendar* years. They are not the same. A single calendar year typically encompasses portions of two different model years.

The following table lists 1950-59 *model-year* production (unless otherwise noted) for the principal series of each major make covered in the text. Cars built for export and chassis built for commercial purposes are excluded. Series are listed in approximate order of introduction and include all body styles originally offered.

	1950	1951	1952	1953	1954	1955	1956	1957	1958	1959
ALLSTATE										
Four			900	425						
Six			666	372						
BUICK										
Special	337,909	164,448	120,153	217,170	190,884	381,249	334,017	220,242	139,213	
Super	251,883	169,226	135,332	190,514	118,630	132,463	80,998	70,259	42,388	
Roadmaster	78,034	66,058	46,217	77,438		64,527	53,427	47,582	14,054	
Skylark				1,690	836					
Century					81,982	158,796	102,189	65,966	37,568	
Limited									7,436	
LeSabre										164,904
Invicta										52,851
Electra										44,185
Electra 225										22,308
CADILLAC										
Series 61	26,770	4,700								
Series 62	59,817	81,842	70,255	84,910	75,193	114,629	127,433	114,087	103,251	70,736
Sixty Special	13,755	18,631	16,110	20,000	16,200	18,300	17,000	24,000	12,900	12,250
Series 75	1,460	2,205	2,200	2,200	1,500	1,916	2,050	2,050	1,532	1,400
Eldorado				532	2,150	3,950	6,050	3,900	1,670	2,295
Eldorado Brougham								400	304	99
DeVille										53,390
CHECKER[1]										
CHEVROLET										
Styleline Special	194,853	175,285	109,506							
Fleetline Special	66,959	9,805								
Styleline DeLuxe	922,982	855,293	671,472							
Fleetline DeLuxe	313,796	189,603	37,164							
One-Fifty				176,579	129,459	125,446	157,294	146,080		
Two-Ten				649,821	524,222	805,309	737,371	651,358		
Bel Air				514,760	486,240	773,238	669,064	702,220	592,000[2]	447,100[2]
Corvette				315	3,640	674	3,467	6,339	9,168	9,670
Delray									178,000[2]	
Biscayne									176,229	311,800[2]
Impala									60,000	473,000[2]
Station Wagon									187,063	214,383
CHRYSLER										
Royal	24,687									
Windsor	112,212	82,764	42,683	32,192	44,527		86,080	48,055	26,975	35,483
Windsor DeLuxe				52,277		98,874				
Saratoga	1,300	28,664	16,835					37,196	18,486	17,479
New Yorker	29,333	34,285	17,914	49,313	20,419		41,140	34,620	17,411	16,326
New Yorker DeLuxe				27,184	34,306	52,177				
Town & Country	700									
Imperial	10,650	17,303	9,780	8,859	5,659					

[1]not available [2]rounded to nearest 100 [3]1951 production includes 1952 (no separate breakout available) [4]includes 1949 models [5]estimated [6]1950-53 production estimated [7]1953 production includes 1954 (no separate breakout available) [8]model-year registrations [9]includes Rambler [10]includes V-8 models [11]total 1957 Studebaker production: 74,438 [12]included with 1950 total

	1950	1951	1952	1953	1954	1955	1956	1957	1958	1959
Crown Imperial	414	440	258	159	100					
"300"						1,725	1,102	2,402	809	690
CLIPPER										
DeLuxe/Super							14,887			
Custom							3,595			
CONTINENTAL										
Mark II							1,325	444		
Mark III									12,550	
CROSLEY	6,792	6,614	2,075							
DESOTO [3]										
DeLuxe	33,328	21,649								
Custom	100,523	123,000								
Powermaster				43,902	19,204					
Firedome				86,502	57,375	77,760	77,905	45,865	17,479	15,076
Fireflite						37,725	31,517	28,340	12,120	9,127
Firesweep								41,269	19,414	20,834
Adventurer							996	1,950	432	687
DODGE [3]										
Wayfarer	75,403	78,404								
"standard"	266,393	417,605		136,675						
Coronet Eight				183,332						
Meadowbrook 6/V-8					15,444					
Coronet 6/V-8					74,401	110,972	142,613	160,979	77,388	96,782
Royal					64,802	76,660	48,780	40,999	15,165	14,807
Custom Royal						89,304	49,293	55,149	25,112	21,206
Station Wagon								30,481	20,196	23,590
EDSEL										
Ranger									24,049	28,418
Pacer									21,292	
Corsair									9,192	8,653
Citation									8,577	
Station Wagon										7,820
FORD										
DeLuxe	388,368	220,618								
Custom	821,181	792,763						192,775	68,145	
Custom 300								355,237	272,726	482,213
Mainline			163,861	305,714	233,680	127,301	164,442			
Customline			402,542	761,662	674,295	471,992	368,653			
Crestline			105,280	180,164	257,967					
Thunderbird						16,155	15,631	21,380	37,892	67,456
Fairlane						626,250	645,306	148,725	118,140	99,789
Fairlane 500								637,162	306,429	79,011
Station Wagon						209,459	214,446	321,170	184,613	269,338
Galaxie										464,336
FRAZER										
"standard"	14,700[4]									
Manhattan	10,020[4]									
HENRY J		81,942	30,585	16,672	1,123					
HUDSON										
Pacemaker	61,752	34,495	7,486							
Super Six	17,246	22,532								
Super Eight	1,074									
Commodore Six	24,605	16,979	1,592							

	1950	1951	1952	1953	1954	1955	1956	1957	1958	1959
Commodore Eight	16,731	14,243	3,125							
Hornet		43,656	35,921	27,208	24,833					
Wasp/Super Wasp			21,876	17,792	11,603	7,201	2,519			
Jet/Super Jet				21,143	14,224					
Italia					20					
Metropolitan						3,000	3000[5]			
Rambler						25,173	5000[5]			
Hornet V-8						5,119	4,772	3,108		
Hornet Six						6,911	3,380			
IMPERIAL										
"standard"						11,258	10,458	18,066	7,063	7,798
Crown (limo)						172	226	36	31	7
Crown								16,851	8,000	8,332
LeBaron								2,640	1,039	1,132
KAISER[6]										
Special	51,000[4]	60,000			3,929					
DeLuxe	43,750[4]	89,000	7,500	7,883						
Virginian			5,579							
Manhattan			19,000	17,957	4,110	1,291				
Carolina				1,182						
Darrin					435					
LINCOLN										
"standard"/Custom	17,489	16,761								
Cosmopolitan	10,701	15,813	8,045	14,122	7,441	3,549				
Capri			10,272	26,640	29,552	23,673	8,791	5,900	6,859	7,929
Premiere							41,531	35,223	10,275	7,851
Continental Mark IV										11,126
MERCURY										
"standard"	293,658	310,387	172,087							
Custom				149,524	85,067	73,688	85,328			
Monterey				156,339	174,238	151,453	105,369	157,528	62,312	89,277
Montclair						104,667	91,434	75,762	20,673	23,602
Medalist							45,812		18,732	
Turnpike Cruiser								16,861		
Station Wagon								36,012	22,302	24,598
Park Lane									9,252	12,523
MUNTZ	28	230[3]		136[7]						
NASH										
Statesman/ Ambassador	171,782[8]	205,307[8]	154,187[9]	121,643[9]	91,121[9]	40,056	22,709	3,561		
Rambler	9,330						10,000[5]			
Healey		104	150	162	90					
Metropolitan					13,095	6,096	9,068	15,317	13,128	22,309
OLDSMOBILE										
Seventy-Six	33,257									
Eighty-Eight	268,412	34,460	18,617	32,800	72,861	222,361	216,019	172,659	146,567	194,102
Ninety-Eight	106,220	100,519	76,244	100,330	93,325	118,626	90,439	79,693	60,815	81,102
Super 88		150,456	118,558	201,332	187,815	242,192	179,000	132,088	88,992	107,660
PACKARD										
Eight	36,471									
Super Eight	4,528									
Custom Eight	1,384									
"200"/"250"		76,002	51,921							

	1950	1951	1952	1953	1954	1955	1956	1957	1958	1959
"300"/Cavalier		15,309	6,705	10,799	2,580					
Patrician 400		9,001	3,975	7,481	2,760	16,333	6,999			
limousines				150	100					
Clipper/Special				33,168	1,882	23,304		4,809		
Clipper DeLuxe				30,715	10,416					
Clipper Super					10,775					
Clipper Custom						15,380				
"standard"				6,668	2,052				2,034	
Executive							2,815			
Caribbean				750	400	500	539			
Hawk									588	
PLYMOUTH										
DeLuxe	260,663									
Special DeLuxe	348,199									
Concord		139,414[3]								
Cambridge		281,201[3]		201,955						
Cranbrook		586,597[3]		444,653						
Plaza					113,265	189,858	106,947	122,259	94,728	
Savoy					195,929	237,621	226,162	247,657	110,117	132,302
Belvedere					148,334	276,515	152,248	280,584	117,531	116,041
Fury							4,485	7,438	5,303	65,257
Suburban							81,792	104,293	116,120	120,802
Sport Fury										23,857
PONTIAC										
Six	115,542	53,748	19,809	38,914	22,670					
Eight	330,887	316,411	251,564	379,705	149,986					
Star Chief					115,088	199,344	123,283	104,476	48,795	68,815
Chieftain 860						138,520	184,232			
Chieftain 870						215,944	97,914			
Chieftain								162,575	128,819	
Super Chief								65,792	48,795	
Bonneville								630	12,240	82,564
Catalina										231,561
RAMBLER										
Six								114,084[10]	NA	242,581
V-8/Rebel V-8									NA	16,399
American									30,640	91,491
Ambassador									14,570	23,769
STUDEBAKER										
Champion	270,604	144,286	101,390	93,807	51,431	50,368				
Commander	72,562	124,280	84,849	76,092	30,499	58,792				
President						24,666				
Six							28,918	[11]	31,195	
259 V-8							30,654	[11]	12,249	
289 V-8							21,819	[11]	18,670	
Golden Hawk							4,071	4,356	878	
Silver Hawk								15,318	7,350	7,788
Lark Six										98,744
Lark Eight										32,334
WILLYS										
Jeepster	5,844	[12]								
Aero-			31,363	41,549	11,717	5,986				